HAUNTED
SPALDING

Ayscoughfee Hall Museum. (Author's collection)

HAUNTED
SPALDING

Gemma King

The
History
Press

'Mystery creates wonder and wonder is the basis of man's desire to understand.'

Neil Armstrong

Suspected mist manifestation of male upper body captured in Cowbit village when spirits were invited to appear in a photograph. Close inspection on computerised image seems to reveal facial detail.

First published 2012

The History Press
The Mill, Brimscombe Port
Stroud, Gloucestershire, GL5 2QG
www.thehistorypress.co.uk

© Gemma King, 2012

The right of Gemma King to be identified as the Author
of this work has been asserted in accordance with the
Copyrights, Designs and Patents Act 1988.

ISBN 978 0 7524 6992 8
Typesetting and origination by The History Press
Printed in Great Britain

Contents

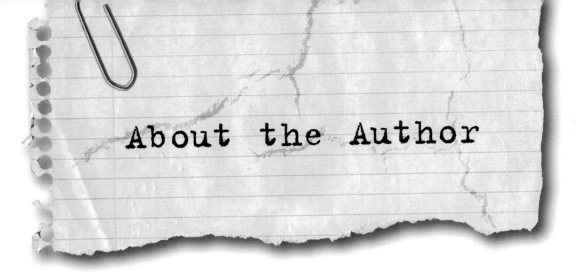

About the Author

GEMMA KING has resided in Spalding for many years. Her interest in the paranormal dates back to her childhood and, at the age of nineteen, her curiosity was further fuelled when she had a ghostly experience of her own. By this time, she had already done much research into the paranormal and the different types of ghost manifestation. Now in her thirties, Gemma has carried out many investigations in Spalding and further afield. She is known locally for her interest in the supernatural and has been invited to give talks about her experiences. Her investigative work is conducted scientifically and objectively with the use of specialist equipment and techniques, and her ultimate aim has always been to capture irrefutable evidence of ghosts. Throughout the course of her investigative work she has been able to offer assistance to people seeking insight or advice in relation to paranormal activity, and has always found this aspect of her work by far the most rewarding.

Gemma King.

Acknowledgements

THIS book would not have been possible had it not been for the valued contributions, co-operation and support from countless people, and I would like to take this opportunity to thank them. Firstly, I would like to give special thanks to my husband Phil and my two children, Mikey (five) and Jasmine (three), for their unwavering patience and encouragement during my busy periods of research, investigating and writing. In addition to his support of my project, Phil has provided crucial assistance with some of my illustrations and in setting up the website. I am very grateful for his invaluable contribution. I would also like to thank my fellow team members in Spalding Paranormal Investigations: Pam Stretton, Stuart Moulder, Chris Joyce and Josh Stretton for their support in this project, their friendship, and for all of the investigations that we have carried out together.

Special thanks go to my parents Lin and Den, my sister Melissa and brother-in-law Daniel, and the rest of my family and close friends, who have always supported my passion for all things paranormal and who have offered so much encouragement over the years. Furthermore, my brother Daniel Watts worked extremely hard on my behalf, filming and putting together a promotional video for the book; big thanks go to him.

Finally, I would like to thank the following people, whose contributions and assistance with research really made this book possible: Julia Knight of Ayscoughfee Hall for her generosity in accommodating my many requests and visits to the building whilst writing this book, for her personal assistance in putting together the historical aspects of the Ayscoughfee feature, and for giving me the privileged opportunity of conducting a paranormal investigation in the building; Councillor Howard Johnson, who was extremely supportive of the investigation work in Ayscoughfee; Geoff Neal (Geoff Neal & Son Dry Cleaners, Bridge Street); Clive Herd (Russel's Café, New Road); Sue Stoker (Royal Mail Cart); John Shores, Dennis Felt, David Jack, Norma Jack, Kerryanne Burton, Joe and Kay Cifaldi (Joe's Restaurant); Andrew and Judy Sadd (Long Sutton & District Civic Society); John Cleary (Spalding Gentlemen's Society); Lauren McFarland; Leanne and Jackie (Chequers Hotel, Holbeach); David Stanbridge (Cley Hall Hotel); Margaret Johnson; Georgie Turp and Natalie Turnbull (Woodlands

Hotel); Mr and Mrs Spencer (Holbeach Sports & Social Club); Geoff Hemsil, Cliff Elsom, Jane Martin (Elsom Cross Printers); Richard Rickerby (String of Horses Inn); Julia Farmer (the Mansion House Hotel, Holbeach); and Zara Foster (the Crown Inn, Surfleet) for her valued support in the fundraising paranormal investigation that took place at the Crown Inn.

All photographs in this publication, unless otherwise stated, are copyright of the author. I have made every effort to contact copyright holders and gain permission for the use of material, but apologise if I have inadvertently missed anyone out.

Introduction

LOCATED in the heart of the Fens, on the site of a former Benedictine monastery, Spalding has developed over the centuries from a shipping town into a busy and vibrant market town. No matter where you are in Spalding or the surrounding area, you are never far away from sites of historical interest and it is therefore no wonder that there is such a wide variety of ghostly phenomena.

In compiling this book, my aim has been to look in detail at paranormal events in the area, including eyewitness accounts of ghost sightings and paranormal experiences. As well as documenting these accounts, I have carried out investigations at some of the locations featured – along with local investigation team SPI (Spalding Paranormal Investigations) – in an attempt to separate fact from folklore. In doing so, I have often managed to gain insight into the unexplainable events taking place, capturing some quite compelling evidence in the process. I have also endeavoured to research the history surrounding the haunted locations featured, as this can often be instrumental in providing clues to the reasons behind paranormal events. Of course, the history of Spalding is a fascinating subject all on its own, but merely touching on it whilst researching particular stories for this book has given me great understanding as to why some of the locations are very haunted indeed. I hope that readers will enjoy the historical aspects of this book as well as the ghostly testimonies from local people, the details of paranormal investigations and the previously unseen photographs of Spalding in times gone by.

Gemma King, 2012

1

Paranormal Investigations

Preparation and Equipment

When my team carry out investigations we use various tools, technology and techniques in order to maximise the possibility of capturing evidence of paranormal activity. We vary our equipment according to the place in question and the kind of activity taking place. In this chapter, I will describe the general investigation process; I hope that this will provide insight for anyone unfamiliar with how the process works.

Motion sensors
Trigger objects
Digital camera
Voice recorder
Air & Laser thermometer
EMF sensor
Torches
Video camera

Investigation equipment. (Author's collection)

Night-Vision Camcorder – We investigate in the dark whenever possible (with the use of torches) as doing this opens up our other senses, making us more aware of unusual smells, movement and sounds. It is also noteworthy that night-vision cameras pick up anomalies such as floating orbs/ mists particularly well. Thermal-imaging cameras are also fantastic in that they clearly show specific areas of cold or hot energy, and have been known to pick up ghostly figures in this way. Sadly, they are very expensive, so our team does not currently have one.

EMF (Electromagnetic Field) Detector – Also known as the KII, this tracks levels of electromagnetic energy. The theory is that spirits use electromagnetic energy to manifest and this is why phenomena such as dipping/flickering lights are associated with ghostly manifestation – because the spirits are draining power from the lights as their energy source. In an ideal investigation, upon encountering this phenomenon you would find an isolated cold spot in the room and, upon holding the EMF meter in that spot, it would light up, showing a higher reading than everywhere else. This is a widely accepted theory in the field of paranormal investigation. That said, random EMF hits which occur during an investigation should be considered objectively, taking into account possible increases in EMF from external sources. A good way to validate EMF hits is to use the meter as a communication tool, inviting the spirits present to come over and touch it (making it clear, of course, that the gadgets you are using cannot hurt them and will simply enable them to communicate). If the machine lights up from green to orange, invite them to take it up to red and keep it on red. Then, when it has been flickering

on red for a few seconds, ask them to step away from the machine – it should then go back to green. If you get to this stage, it is highly possible that you are communicating with an 'intelligent' spirit and you can continue to use the tool to seek further proof – perhaps even inviting them to interact with the machine, to answer 'yes' or 'no' to your questions.

EMF meters are also a good tool for debunking theories of paranormal activity, and this is because they were originally used by building contractors/engineers to locate dangerously high levels of energy in buildings; if cables are not properly insulated or there are too many strong sources of the energy in one place, dangerous levels of EMF are emitted, creating what is sometimes referred to as a 'fear cage'. When exposed to the area in question for prolonged periods of time, a person may suffer symptoms such as feelings of paranoia and anxiety, visual and aural hallucinations, nausea, or even skin irritation – all of which are frequently associated with paranormal activity. In other words, a person could think that they have a resident ghost when they don't. Many people would seek comfort in the knowledge that the solution to their 'paranormal activity' merely involves insulating cables or moving household appliances to minimise their exposure to the EMF!

Thermometer – This picks up random hot or cold spots. There are two types of thermometer that can be used on investigations: laser thermometers (which measure surface temperatures) or air thermometers (which are good for investigating cold spots). Sometimes an investigator will invite spirits to drop the temperature by a specified number of degrees. This is helpful when looking for evidence of intellectual spirit energies – especially when reviewed in conjunction with other evidence, such as EMF hits and EVP (electronic voice phenomena).

Digital Voice Recorder – This is my favourite piece of equipment as it records sounds undetectable to the human ear, known as EVP. The theory is that spirit voices can only be heard on a very low frequency – a frequency only detectable to certain animals – and it is often the case that you investigate a place that seems quite inactive at the time but when you play back the audio recording it will tell a different story, picking up voices and sounds. The original voice recorders were not digital; this has caused much debate over the years as it was frequently alleged by sceptics that the voices heard were not spirit voices but radio interference. Of course, this was always strongly refuted by believers in the phenomenon, given that the voices recorded often belonged to children or the elderly – not the kind of voices that you would expect to hear on a radio. Also, the voices picked up would often be responding to specific questions asked by the investigator. Thankfully, the progression to digital technology in recent years has greatly reduced white noise, meaning that interference from radio waves is now highly unlikely. When recording EVP, it is important to minimise noise contamination from the environment; it is always surprising how loud people's footsteps sound on playback, and I have often found that heavy footsteps can make suspected EVP recordings difficult to decipher!

Environment Meter – This device takes 'base readings' around the investigation site, showing the humidity, sound levels and the level of electromagnetic energy naturally present in the environment. This means that once we begin the investigation we can easily see anomalies/remote fluctuations that occur, such as sudden temperature drops or high levels of electromagnetic energy in specific areas.

Digital Camera – Cameras are very good at picking up orbs, mists and shadows in photographs. I always explain my equipment during usage to make sure that spirits do not feel threatened by it and, in respect of the camera, I invite them to appear in my photographs. This can produce some very strange anomalies. Whilst orbs are not generally accepted as ghost images (because they commonly appear in photographs and do not take human form), they are still widely regarded as a sign of spirit manifestation. It is said to take a lot of energy for a spirit to manifest in full human form, so revealing themselves as an orb might be the easiest way of making themselves visible to us. Sceptics would argue that orbs are simply dust particles; however, even though I am very objective in my investigative thought processes, I struggle to find an explanation for orbs which are clearly too big or bright to be 'dust' – and they seem to appear in front of the camera upon request! Large, bright orbs have also been caught on film. Some orbs, if examined very closely on photographs, appear to have faces in them and I find this most intriguing. Although my ultimate photography objective is to capture a full body apparition, I will continue to explore the orb phenomenon with much interest. Another theory which suggests that orbs are spiritual beings has derived from accounts of near-death experiences, where people claim to have become an orb of light upon leaving their physical body and been greeted by other orbs of light (recognisable to them as family members). So could there be some truth in the orb theory? No one has the answer, but it will always be an interesting debate.

Torch — This is essential, as paranormal investigations usually take place at night. Torches which have a button on the back are useful, because you can place them in the middle of the floor and invite spirits to turn them off.

Trigger Objects — I use trigger objects (items which would be of interest to the spirit) to encourage interaction during the investigation. For example, if I am trying to engage with children I use toys, for a spirit that leaves a cigar smell I use a cigar, and for a monk I use a cross. After placing the trigger objects on a piece of paper and drawing round them, you invite the spirits to take them. In the case of the toys (usually light-weight things that can easily be moved, such as a rolling ball) I invite the children to play with them. If any trigger objects are moved during an investigation, and this is caught on camera, it is fantastic evidence of paranormal activity — as long as you can prove it was not just a draught!

Motion Sensors — It is intriguing if trigger objects are interfered with but the motion sensors do not react. Of course, it is also exciting if they *do* react to movement when there is no one in that room.

Walkie-Talkies — These are useful when investigating a large area where the team splits into pairs to do separate vigils. It is worth mentioning that I don't believe people should investigate on their own — not only because it's unsafe fumbling around an unfamiliar place in the dark, but also because it is better for validation pur-

poses if at least two people have the same paranormal experience simultaneously.

Flour/Talc — If there is an area where foot-steps are frequently heard, then flour or talc can be used to capture footprints. The flour should be isolated so as not to be contaminated by other footprints, although prints from anyone present at the investigation can easily be dismissed. I recently investigated a location where handprints were mysteriously appearing on one particular mirror — I used talc in that case to try to capture some evidence.

Séances

I do not have any psychic ability, and investigate by using technology to try to capture hard evidence of paranormal activity. However, the team I work with do conduct séances using a board and glass and, since participating myself, I have become truly intrigued by them.

What I like most about the séances is that they do not seem to have any scientific explanation. One theory suggests that it is the power of the mind that moves the glass to spell words. However, even if this was possible, in instances where no one around the table knows anyone else, I cannot see how this could be the case — given the very specific information that comes through, directed at just one person.

What I also love is the fact that séances can be pretty accurate, and everybody can see and feel the experience. The direct communication with spirit entities means that séances can provide answers on the paranormal activity in people's homes or places of work, and can also help resolve situations where unhappy spirits are making the occupants of a building feel

Séance. Pictured from left to right: Gemma King, Chris Joyce, Stuart Moulder, Pam Stretton. (Author's collection)

uncomfortable. One such case springs to mind, where a resident spirit child came through to talk to the owner of a place we were investigating. It transpired that she had been trying to get their attention because she did not like the loud chimes on the clocks, which she found scary. The owner had many clocks and they covered the walls in one particular room. He agreed to turn some off, which provided a resolution and a positive outcome for everyone concerned.

On some occasions during a séance, we encounter a spirit that asks for our help because they are grounded – i.e. unable to move on – and this can happen for a number of different reasons. Through careful questioning, we are often able to work out the reason and assist them in moving on. I do not know how this works, but it does work, and the feeling when it happens is immensely comforting and emotional for everyone. It is good to know that through séances we are seemingly able to assist

trapped energies. Scientific though I am, I do believe in séances and the possibility that we can help people, here and in spirit, which reinforces my passion and belief in this investigative tool.

Whilst the use of the Ouija board is controversial, I feel this negative perception is often based on movies or television programmes, where their use invariably lends itself to some kind of horrific drama. It could also partly be due to the experiences of individuals who used them in previous decades, when the boards were sold in shops as a recreational toy. I have no doubt that many people who have used the Ouija board over the years have not fully understood or respected the seriousness of this method of communication with spirits, and as such may not have conducted themselves appropriately. The séances that are conducted by my paranormal investigation team are protected by an opening and closing-down prayer; no one under the influence of alcohol is ever allowed to participate; and anyone that does take part must remain respectful to any spirit energies that come through.

Members of my team have been conducting séances for many years and have never had a negative experience. That said, it is crucial that people know how to respond appropriately to the unpredictable spirit communications during a séance. It is not something to partake in lightly and I would certainly not recommend anyone doing it unless they are with an experienced individual.

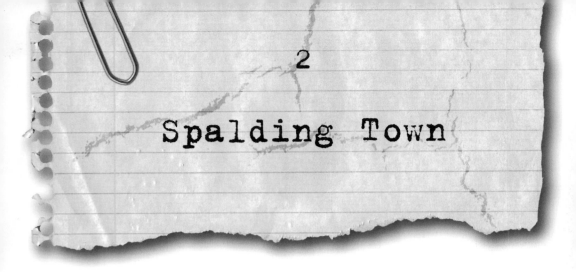

2

Spalding Town

Cley Hall Hotel, High Street

Cley Hall was built as a family home in 1754 by Theophilus Buckworth. It was inherited by his grandson, Theophilus Fairfax Johnson, son of Revd Maurice Johnson of Ayscoughfee Hall. The hall remained in the Buckworth/Johnson family until sometime after 1835 and, whilst details of ownership immediately after this are unclear, records do show that a farmer by the name of Walpole Allen was the registered owner in 1861. He resided at the house with his mother initially, then later his wife Emma. In 1964 a new owner wanted to demolish the building to make way for a new building project – however, its future was saved by a preservation order in 1968, and it was lovingly restored and transformed into an art gallery. In 1974, new owners opened it as a restaurant and bar, then in 1980 it finally became a hotel.

The most notable ghostly sighting occurred a few years prior to the writing of this book. The gentleman concerned began by telling me that he had never previously been a believer in ghosts, but his experience at Cley Hall had completely changed that. He had been employed as a decorator to carry out some work on the premises and had been working by himself in the front lounge for a week or so. On the day in question, he was doing some panel work and, having removed the large gilded mirror from the wall above the fireplace and closed both lounge doors, he set about working on one of the panels. Suddenly, he became aware of a movement in the room. Looking up, he saw a man with curly white hair, aged between fifty and sixty, dressed in a red waist-length jacket, a white ruffled shirt, breeches and shiny black shoes with silver buckles. The man seemingly appeared from one of the wall panels; the decorator watched, rather stunned, as the man from the past briskly walked through the room, disappearing through the panel in the opposite wall. On the other side of this wall is the hallway, and the contractor left the room to follow him. He watched, a bit shocked, as the mysterious figure walked through a closed door and then disappeared, without a trace.

He knew that he had not imagined this event and was not only baffled but slightly shaken by it, although not frightened. He said that the gentleman, whilst pale in appearance, was not transparent. When he

Cley Hall Hotel. (Author's collection)

Cley Hall for many years when it was her family home), neither was able to offer any further insight into this strange event. They had not experienced or been informed of any similar occurrences during their time in the building. However, I did speak with another lady, who informed me that when she had worked at Cley Hall Hotel in previous years, a shadowy figure had been seen by staff downstairs in the bar area. She also informed me that when working upstairs she would often hear the sound of disembodied footsteps. When hearing these sounds she was usually alone in the building and therefore could never find an explanation for them. It was widely accepted by staff that the building was haunted, although the ghosts never interacted with anyone.

These testimonies are of great interest to me and I feel that the appearance of the gentleman apparition has all the hallmarks of a residual ghost – i.e. not an intelligent spirit but a ghostly apparition, deriving from energy of a past event, which has become contained in the fabric of the building. Disembodied footsteps can also be residual sounds. Residual ghosts have no awareness so would never engage in communication – they are merely a visual spectacle. When they appear they are often walking through walls or dusting furniture that is no longer there – following the routines from their life. They will always appear in the same location, repeating the same motions. There is a theory that some building materials – such as stone, limestone, slate or iron nails – are able to store an event in a similar way to a videotape, and 'play it back' at a later stage; this is the best way to describe a residual ghost. The aforementioned building materials are comparable to a videotape because of their similar components – videotapes are made

walked through the room there was no sound at all – no rustle of clothing or sound of footsteps. Also, the gentleman seemed unaware of the decorator's presence, neither looking at nor acknowledging him.

With the current owner of Cley Hall Hotel, I retraced the route taken by the ghostly gentleman. In the place where the apparition walked through the wall, there are remnants of a former door frame. There is no sign of the door frame on the lounge side of the wall, but in the hallway the door frame is visible all the way down to ground level. Records show that there was indeed previously a door there which was subsequently blocked off.

I was very keen to research this story and find other testimonies of paranormal activity connected with the building. However, when I spoke with the current owner of Cley Hall Hotel, and also a lady called Margaret Johnson (who resided at

Above *The front lounge at Cley Hall Hotel. The apparition walked through the right wall, approximately where the picture is seen hanging.*

Right *The apparition emerged through the wall on the left of the picture, within the remnants of the old door frame. (Author's collection)*

of special material that has been oxidised or rusted in order to capture and store the information. Whilst the topic is still heavily debated and researched, it is generally accepted that many disembodied sounds and ghostly sightings can be attributed to this phenomenon.

It is said that building work can be a catalyst for many types of paranormal activity, even 'intelligent' activity, and it is possible in this case that the building work on the panels somehow disturbed the energy and triggered the playback. This could certainly explain why no previous sightings of the gentleman had been reported.

Residual Ghosts and Acoustic Archaeology

When I think about residual ghosts and energies, I relate it to a study that has been carried out in Egypt whereby sounds of the past have been uncovered and 'played back' from ancient pottery. The system used to play back the sound is surprisingly simple: a crystal cartridge is connected to a pair of inexpensive headphones and needles are fitted at the other end of the cartridge. A piece of pottery, such as a vase, is then placed on a turntable and the 'needle' (a thin piece of wood) is manually placed upon the pottery while it turns. The sounds are then picked up from the grooves, like on a record. The ancient sounds heard in some experiments have included chattering, laughter and sometimes even singing; these sounds will have been captured within the fabric of the items while they were being made all those years ago. Whilst I can only speculate about the scientific theories behind residual energy, it is noteworthy that energy cannot be destroyed. I think there are similarities in the properties of residual ghost energy, disembodied sounds and the acoustic archaeology experiments and, who knows, one day scientists may be able to fully explain them all.

Joe's Restaurant, Double Street

Ever since Joe Cifaldi and his wife Kay opened their restaurant on Double Street in 2009, many unusual occurrences have been reported by staff. Beautifully renovated from what was formerly the Spalding Fire Brigade building, this contemporary restaurant has seen all kinds of unexplain-

Joe's Restaurant. (Author's collection)

able phenomena, from disembodied voices to interference with the kitchen appliances.

Mr and Mrs Cifaldi informed me that the first thing they noticed was the sound of voices. However, as time progressed many other events occurred – some quite frightening, if only because of their sudden and unexpected nature. On one occasion, staff member Kerry was washing up in the kitchen when she became aware of what she thought was a large white plate flying towards her. She flinched and ducked but quickly realised that it was not a plate at all, but a large white orb of light, which disappeared on impact with her. This left her very shaken. Quite a few of the strange occurrences have affected Kerry, who spent a lot of time working in the restaurant until she left to have a baby. The first thing she recalled was the name calling; quite frequently, she would hear someone shouting her name, sometimes very loudly, and it was always a voice that she recognised as belonging to a colleague. When she went to find that person, it would always transpire that no one had called her at all and no one else had heard the voice. This happened many times, and has happened to several other staff members as

Shelf where glass has unexplainably and quite methodically fallen, smashing on the floor.

fact that she would not have been able to reach the pen, told Kerry that she was definitely not responsible.

Whilst Kerry has had many strange experiences in the restaurant, she is by no means the only one. Most of the staff have experienced phenomena at some stage. On one occasion, Joe was in the toilet block when he heard the sound of glasses smashing onto the floor. He ran out to the bar area and was shocked to see two of the waitresses watching in dismay as glasses fell off the shelf behind the bar, one by one. Joe and his wife are not believers in the paranormal, but were shocked by this event because it seemed scientifically impossible for the glasses to be falling in that manner – slowly, one by one.

On a personal note, I am always far more intrigued by testimonies that come from non-believers; they are more objective and generally try to rationalise an experience, looking for other possible causes. After all, an event can only truly be described as 'paranormal' if there is no scientific explanation, and this is why the process of 'debunking' is a crucial part of investigation work.

After this strange experience, Joe examined the shelf carefully and tipped it up in different ways, trying to recreate the phenomenon. He was looking for a fault with the shelf, with a view to establishing the cause. However, he was unable to make the glasses fall again in the gradual and seemingly controlled way that they had fallen, and this left him extremely baffled. Another incident also involved the glasses: Kerry was chatting to Joe's daughter (at a time when the restaurant was empty) when they suddenly became aware of a screeching sound – like chalk on a blackboard. Upon following the noise, they could see that the champagne glasses were moving along the glass shelf behind them – seemingly on

well; it is as though the spirit presence is imitating various people's voices and calling for assistance as a prank.

Kerry often felt a sensation of someone brushing past her, or heard talking in her ear. On one occasion, she was standing at the bar talking to a little girl and, as she turned around and walked away, the pen that she had been writing with launched itself from the diary pad where it had been placed and slid across the floor. There was no reason for this to happen and nothing that the pen could have caught on. Kerry looked at the little girl, suspecting that she had thrown the pen; however, the bemused look on the girl's face, together with the their own. Given the fact that there were other unexplainable events taking place in the restaurant – the sound of disembodied voices, objects being moved, a sighting of an apparition going into the store room, a dark shadowy figure walking through the kitchen, and the numerous experiences seen and felt by different staff members – this began to play on the owners' minds. A formerly sceptical Joe was compelled to consider the likelihood of a ghostly presence in the building.

The spirit at Joe's Restaurant seems intent on making his presence felt in many different ways, and new incidents of paranormal activity are frequently being noted. For instance, he commonly seems to interfere with kitchen appliances. One morning, Joe arrived at the restaurant to discover the pizza oven was switched on – but it had been checked and confirmed to be off when the building was locked up the previous night. The staff carefully check everything before they close the restaurant at night, given the number of times that appliances appear to have been tampered with. Other such events include the extractor fans (which are operated by a dial that has to be turned all the way down to the 'off' position) all being turned off, and a freezer being switched off during the night, causing all of the food inside to defrost.

Since my initial interview with the staff at Joe's, a member of staff has reported seeing the black figure of a man walking past the back door. However, when the employee opened the door to check outside, there was no sign of anyone – and no

Inside Joe's Restaurant. The paranormal activity seems to be most concentrated in the rear right-hand corner of the restaurant, the bar area, and in the kitchen which is located further back. (Author's collection)

Washing-up area in the kitchen, where a large white ball of light flew at a member of staff and disappeared upon impact. Close to this area is the back door, where a shadowy figure was seen walking past. (Author's collection)

means of entering or leaving the premises, as the compound was locked at the time.

The Cifaldi family concluded their interview by telling me that they are not concerned by the spirit, whom they have affectionately named 'Fred' as, whilst he does make his presence felt, he never hurts anyone, and the encounters that the staff have described as frightening were only considered so because they were sudden and unexpected.

Looking back at the history of the building, Spalding Fire Brigade was based there until 1984, and then it was occupied until approximately 2002 by St John Ambulance. Following a large fire on the premises, the building remained unoccupied for a considerable number of years, before Mr and Mrs Cifaldi opened their restaurant in 2009. I was mindful during the interview with Joe that when buildings are renovated, or stand unoccupied for a long period of time, this can be a catalyst for paranormal activity. However, Joe informed me that reports of strange activity in the building actually date

back many years, to when the building was occupied by the fire brigade. Upon questioning this with much interest, Joe told me that when the restaurant had been opened for one year, they had hosted an anniversary celebration dinner and invited members of the former fire brigade to attend. On that evening, one of the firemen had asked Joe if he had experienced anything unusual in the building. When Joe had replied 'Yes', the fireman had explained that it was very 'active' when it was occupied by them. The crew and Joe spent the evening sharing some of their experiences.

Before Joe's Restaurant – The Experiences of Spalding Fire Brigade

I was keen to speak with former fire-brigade crew members about their experiences in the building and was put in touch with former Sub Fire Officer John Shores, who served with Spalding Fire Brigade from 1962. John told me that at the back of the station, above the watch room, was a recreational room with a snooker table. The crew members felt that a ghostly presence focused on this room. The most notable thing was that it was always cold – no matter how many heaters they put in there. There was also a very oppressive atmosphere and, whilst they were always reluctant to admit it to one another, the crew really disliked going up there alone. What they disliked more than anything was the night watch, as just a couple of officers would be present. During the night, some crew members would feel extremely uncomfortable in the building, hearing strange sounds. Some of the noises were simply put down to the age of the building; however, on one occasion a strange noise led them to inves-

Above *Spalding Fire Crew pictured outside the old fire station in 1981. (Courtesy of Dennis Felt and Spalding Gentlemen's Society)*

Right *This picture, taken on 26 June 1923, shows the carpenter's workshop before it became the site of the fire brigade. (Courtesy of Dennis Felt and Spalding Gentlemen's Society)*

tigate the recreation room. They had heard the sound of a heavy object dropping and, upon entering the room, they noticed that one of the snooker balls had found its way out of the corner pocket on the snooker table, dropped down, and was rolling along the floor. No one had been up there at the time and they knew that the balls had all previously been secure in the nets (which were not damaged in any way).

The fire crew were aware that before the Spalding Fire Brigade was established on the Double Street site in 1935, that building had been occupied by a carpenter who had taken his own life. It is said that the recreation room was the location of that terrible tragedy. I have opted not to publish his name, but over the years many people have suspected that the spirit of that gentleman may still be making his presence felt.

New Look, Market Place

Some staff at the New Look store have heard unexplained noises, as though someone is walking around upstairs. One member of staff saw a shadowy figure walking past her up there. An apparition of a little girl has also been seen, accompanied by a very 'cold' feeling.

Hedonism hair salon. (Author's collection)

Hedonism, Broad Street

Currently a contemporary hair salon, former occupants of this building on Broad Street have noted the sound of little footsteps running about upstairs. A visitor to the building, who claimed to have ability as a medium, is said to have connected with the spirit presence of a little girl.

Neat & Tidy, Station Street

Some staff at this hair salon have heard their names being called by a mysterious disembodied female voice.

Lamb & Flag, High Road

The owners of this public house have noticed strange phenomena since the first night they occupied the building, when music could be heard inside – from no known source. This continued intermittently throughout the night as the landlord periodically explored the building and car park. Baffled, he concluded that the music had definitely been coming from inside the building but he couldn't establish exactly where. On another occasion, the landlord was putting up shelves in the upstairs kitchen when he heard a child's voice say, 'Hello there, how are you doing?' The family dog, with him upstairs, was jumping up at the stair gate and wagging its tail, as though someone was standing there. At this time, the owner was preoccupied with his DIY, and assumed his youngest son had spoken to him. However, a few moments later he went downstairs and asked his son what he had wanted – it transpired that his son, who had been in a completely different part of the building, had not been upstairs at all.

Something else that both the landlord and landlady have noticed over time is that objects keep going missing or being moved; this is frequently the subject of banter between the couple, who blame each other when the incidents occur. Sometimes when the couple sit down to have a cup of tea together, one of them will feel a warm sensation on their lap, which feels like a child is sitting there. After a while, the sensation will stop and

The Lamb & Flag public house. (Author's collection)

then occur on the other person's lap. The owners of the Lamb & Flag say that they are not uncomfortable at all with the unusual occurrences in their pub, as none are ever unpleasant and they love the idea that a spirit child could be finding happiness and comfort around them.

The Station Gates, Winsover Road

Former staff of this currently disused pub can recall ghostly events such as the bar hatch falling down with no obvious cause, when it had been leaning back against the wall; light bulbs being moved from one fitting to another; and, on one disturbing occasion, a tile shooting from the wall in the gentlemen's toilets, flying across the room and hitting a man on the head. Despite the tile incident, the ghost was generally considered friendly and had been given the name Isabelle by staff.

House, Albion Street

A residential property on this street has been visited by the ghost of a First World War soldier. The sighting of the man was reported by a little boy, who told his parents that he did not want to go in the bathroom because there was already someone in there. When questioned further, he described the soldier – but little did he know that, during the First World War, a makeshift hospital was established in Willesby House on Albion Street. Could this have been the spirit of an ex-patient?

The Ship Albion Inn, Albion Street

Dating back to the early 1700s, the Ship Albion Inn has long been a fixture on Albion Street. It was a well-known and very busy meeting place for sailors when Spalding was a shipping town, and there was a lot of trade and traffic on the river in the 1700s and 1800s. In the early 1900s, river traffic started to decline dramatically; despite this, the Ship Albion Inn has always celebrated its connection with seafaring folk. Today it is a modern pub and

The Ship Albion Inn. (Author's collection)

Albion Street. (Author's collection)

restaurant enjoyed by the locals, but the paranormal activity experienced by staff is perhaps an indication that the roving sailors' connection with the place is as strong now as it was all those years ago.

A member of the public reported the following shocking sighting of an apparition. He had been sitting at the bar with his girlfriend, admiring the architecture, showing much interest in the history of the building and asking lots of questions. When he asked about the cellar and wanted to have a look, the landlady happily obliged, so he went down for a quick peek. Upon his return, the customer said, 'Did you know that there's someone in the cellar? There is a man down there and he told me his name is Frank.' The landlady knew that no one was in the cellar and so was rather baffled by this revelation.

The landlady herself frequently hears whistling in the pub and believes she has seen floating orbs of light in the dining area. On my visit to the pub I took some of my technical gadgetry, as I always do, and was surprised by some of the readings that I got on my EMF detector. Around the cushioned seating at one particular table, the EMF lights were fully illuminating with no explainable source – as though someone, or perhaps more than one person, was sitting around the table. I also invited 'Frank' to illuminate the EMF lights on my way down into the cellar, and got a responsive illumination on the steps – again with no obvious source.

The staff at the Ship Albion Inn are very happy to share their building with Frank, and they frequently talk to him so he knows that his presence is welcome.

The restaurant at the Ship Albion Inn, where the landlady has reported seeing floating orbs and hearing disembodied whistling. (Author's collection)

15 New Road

Currently used as a commercial property, 15 New Road has been connected to the Herd family of Spalding since 1914, when Mrs Herd's grandmother took up residence. Since that time, three generations of the family have resided there, including Mrs Herd herself, and it would seem that the progressive family tie to the building has been very relevant in this unusual ghost story.

Throughout the generations, members of the family have reported seeing the apparition of a smartly dressed gentleman, wearing top hat and tails and carrying a black cane, walking through their backyard. He has been seen on numerous occasions over the years, entering their garden through the garden wall, then walking across the yard and disappearing into an outbuilding. What is especially eerie is that usually, within days of him being witnessed, there is a death in the family.

The ghost was first seen by Mrs Herd's grandmother and it preceded the death of *her* grandmother. When I spoke with Mrs Herd about her own experiences, she recalled seeing him in 1956 – just before her grandfather died – and again in 1966 just before her grandmother died.

Mrs Herd's daughter Claire saw the gentleman just before the death of her grandmother; this was the most recent sighting. The family members have consistently described him as 'gentry' in appearance and also reminiscent of an undertaker that worked locally many years ago. They have all given exactly the same description of his clothing. No one has ever seen his face in detail but they have estimated his age at between forty and fifty. There is no rustle of his clothing or sound of his footsteps, and he has never uttered a word. On one occasion though, as recalled by Mrs Herd's son Dean, the ghostly gentleman paused en route to the outbuilding and turned to look at him. After a brief unspoken exchange between them, the enigmatic gentleman continued on his usual route, disappearing into the remains of a shed. Dean was not frightened by the experience and the family are generally not afraid of the gentleman.

Whilst this seems to have all the hallmarks of a residual ghost, in that the gentleman walks through walls, taking exactly the same route each time and not making a sound, it is particularly intriguing that he acknowledged Dean's presence by pausing to look at him. This leads me to believe it could be an intelligent spirit. The timing of the sightings is also very bizarre. Is it just coincidence, or is there a spirit gentleman watching over the family – perhaps guiding them when they pass over to the spirit world?

Georgian House, London Road

The existence of this beautiful Georgian house can be traced back as far as 1703. Over the years, the family there have encountered numerous spirit presences – including a monk, believed to be linked with the Benedictine priory that occupied a large area of the town centuries ago.

The most notable spirit presence, however, has been the apparition of a little girl, approximately seven years of age, who has blonde hair in ringlets and wears a pink pinafore. She has been seen and sensed many times by the family, playing in the back bedroom and also in the garden. One family member who has probably seen her more than most is Claire, who grew up in the house and recalls having an 'imaginary

Georgian House. (Author's collection)

friend' as a child; but it would not be until years later that she would uncover the full story behind the spirit girl.

It is believed that the little girl lived in this house many years ago but, in a tragic accident, fell down the stairs and broke her neck. Concerned for the welfare of the spirit girl, the family held a séance in an attempt to establish whether she needed any help. During the séance they managed to connect with her and she told them that she was looking for her mummy. The family were naturally troubled to learn that she was in need of help; however, much to their relief, the little girl was reunited with her family while the séance was ongoing and she is now happy. She still visits the property from time to time and apparently also visits Claire, who is now living at a different address. She makes her presence known by moving objects about and 'playing games'. It would seem that she has formed a special attachment to Claire following their childhood friendship, and Claire speaks very affectionately of her.

The Ivy Wall, New Road

This stylish Wetherspoons public house and restaurant opened in April 2005, following a detailed study of the site which consisted of an archaeological excavation arranged by Wetherspoons. The building dates back to the medieval period, when the river Westlode would have flowed along New Road. Many fascinating artefacts, thought to date from the seventeenth century, were uncovered during the project – including pottery, clay piping and tankards. This led archaeologists to the conclusion that at some stage in a previous century a pub would have occupied the site, just as it does today.

In 1900 the site was occupied by a yeast agent, and in more recent years a garage. Given the extensive history of the site, it is perhaps unsurprising that the Ivy Wall is thought to have a resident ghost. The experiences of staff to date seem to centre around one specific area of the building: the upstairs toilets. One former member of staff apparently used four old spoons to securely prop the door open whilst cleaning – and on many occasions the door would close, seemingly on its own. She would then find the four spoons laid out in a neat line towards the door. The toilets have also been known to flush on their own.

On one occasion, a member of staff was approached by a little boy who told her that a 'scary man' was chasing him upstairs – from the boys' toilets to the girls' toilets. The boy said that this happened every time he came out of the toilet. Concerned staff quizzed the little boy further and it transpired that no one else could see the man; the boy's mother commented that he could often see spirit people. It would be a little irrational to assume that there was a spirit man in this area based on one testimony alone; however, a woman has also claimed to have connected with a spirit gentleman upstairs – although no specific details have been confirmed.

The Ivy Wall. (Author's collection)

Artefacts from the archaeological investigation displayed on the wall, including ancient pottery dating back as far as the seventeenth century. (Author's collection)

Staff members have also commented that objects have randomly dropped on the floor upstairs. Employees have even seen 'someone', thought to be a spirit gentleman, in that area; but there has been no firm description of him. One theory put forward by a spiritual woman claiming to be connecting with the gentleman is that he was there many centuries ago to protect the land. Whatever the reason for his presence, I will be looking around every corner next time I go upstairs at the Ivy Wall!

The Punch Bowl, New Road

The Punch Bowl is one of the few pubs in Spalding that still stands proud with its original name, character and individuality in the town centre. While researching this pub, I was able to trace its existence as far back as 1792. Naturally, given its age, there are plenty of unusual creaks and bumps in the night, but the current landlord feels that not all of the unusual noises and strange events are so easy to explain away.

On several occasions, the staff have noticed that there is no beer coming through the system; upon checking, they have realised that all of the pumps in the cellar have been mysteriously disconnected; the gas is also sometimes disconnected. The current owner of the Punch Bowl actually lives there and he has found this phenomenon quite baffling. Another thing he has noticed is that sometimes the alarms downstairs go off for no reason, and this can coincide with certain strange sounds. Quite often he has to go downstairs in the middle of the night to investigate the noises, but he is never able to find an explanation. One morning he went downstairs to find that a door, which had been locked from the inside with a padlock, was completely open. The padlock had not been forcibly interfered with and was just hanging on the door. The owner was the only person who had access to the keys for that padlock and it could only have been opened from the inside.

The Red Lion Hotel, Market Place

A fixture on Market Place since the 1700s, this family-run hotel has been a hive of activity for centuries. When I heard about some of the spooky and unexplainable events that have taken place inside, I was very keen to meet the staff and find out more. What struck me upon entering the hotel is that you can feel the past in the atmosphere – and even when I was wandering around by myself taking photographs, I did not feel alone.

The first testimony of paranormal activity came from a gentleman who has worked in the hotel for four years. Recalling his time as a night receptionist, he informed me that when all was quiet, around 3 a.m., he would take a tea

The Punch Bowl. (Author's collection)

Two views of the Red Lion Hotel: one from 2011 and one from the early 1900s. (Early picture courtesy of the Red Lion Hotel)

break; whilst sitting in the bar area drinking his tea, items of furniture would move about. He also said that, out of the corner of his eye, he would see shadows appear and seemingly walk past. He was used to people locking themselves out or needing assistance in some way, but these particular shadowy people would walk past making no sound at all (which is unusual, and in fact impossible, for such an old creaky building) and they would then disappear into a wall. He would check inside and outside, looking for the person he had seen, but never found a trace of anyone. Disembodied footsteps have also been heard by several members of staff. Notably,

the hotel has been considerably renovated on the inside over the years – once in 1929 and again in the 1980s – and this process involved walls being moved. Based on this, there is a possibility that the figures and footsteps may be residual energy rather than a spirit. That said, there have been many other incidents reported ...

The most unusual phenomenon in the Red Lion Hotel is the phantom maid in Room 28. No one has ever reported seeing the maid but several guests have woken up in the morning to find a tray on the end of their bed. Furthermore, this mysterious entity runs baths for people – guests will leave the room and return later to find either a complete bath ready for them or running taps.

Another member of staff informed me that on Christmas Eve 2010, he and some colleagues were staying over in the Market Room (on the first floor to the right as you look at the building). It was between 2 a.m. and 3 a.m. and the building was empty. Suddenly, they heard a loud crash coming from nearby. Strangely, upon inspection, they found that nothing was out of place anywhere. The staff are no longer surprised when incidents of this nature occur as they hear many unexplainable sounds throughout the building and have come to expect it – although some of the noises do make them jump!

One member of the family that runs the hotel has had a long connection with the building and even resided there at one stage. He informed me that when he did live there, in Room 15, he would frequently hear footsteps walking up and down the corridor outside the room – at

times when he was sure no one was around. He also recalled an eerie occasion when he was down in the cellar and felt someone push him – the force of this was so strong that he fell down over the barrel he was standing over. He initially thought it was a colleague joking around, but was dismayed to turn around and see no one there at all.

After speaking with several different members of staff, it became clear that the spirit residents at the Red Lion Hotel like to interact with objects; I also learned that things have been broken. One of the bar staff recalled two incidents involving breaking glass. In one case, a drink had been placed in the centre of the bar and the barman looked on, amazed and baffled, as the glass slid along the bar towards the right, completely on its own. When it reached the end of the bar it didn't stop – it fell straight off the end and smashed to pieces on the floor. To this day, the staff are unable to understand how that could have happened.

1938 view of the pub, known then as the Mail Cart. (Courtesy of Sue Stoker)

The other incident involved two expensive vases. The vases were 2ft in height and had been positioned just a few steps apart on the landing – where the stairs veer round to the right, leading up to the guests' rooms. At this time there was no door separating the pub area from the stairs and there was no carpet down – just wooden flooring. A singer/guitarist was entertaining the locals with some Irish protest songs, and during his song one of the vases fell, with considerable force, off the landing and smashed into thousands of pieces on the floor in the pub. The vases were very precious to the owners so this breakage caused much concern. Staff immediately ran to the scene to find out who was responsible but, upon checking the stairs and corridors, no one was anywhere to be seen. As they contemplated the clean-up operation, the singer resumed his song – but once again the melodic atmosphere was to be short-lived. Within moments, the second vase also came crashing down the stairs, smashing to pieces on the wooden floor. It was abundantly clear this time that no individual was anywhere near the vase and everyone in the pub found it quite bizarre. Naturally, the owners of the hotel were devastated at the loss of both their precious vases. After this incident, the guitar player refused to entertain the locals again. He suspected that there might be a resident spirit in the hotel who did not care much for his music, and he didn't want to risk anything else getting broken!

As I walked around the Red Lion Hotel, my EMF detector was quite active on the stairs, lighting up to orange. It remained on orange from the height of my waist, all the way down to the floor. I could not trace a source for this but it did seem to go off quite a lot on the stairs and along the corridor (but always just to waist height). When I stood outside Room 28 I felt a rush of cold air around my legs. Furthermore, when I played back the audio from my walk along the corridor, I could hear another set of footsteps – but those footsteps were clunking on wood as though there was no carpet – and they did not have soft heels like my Ugg boots! This was bizarre to hear on playback, as I know that I was completely alone in that part of the building at the time of recording. Could there have been a spirit or two following me around the hotel?

Royal Mail Cart

The Royal Mail Cart public house was initially constructed in 1843 as a family home. The exact history is sketchy but it is clear from old photographs showing progressive alterations to the building that it used to be called the Mail Cart Inn. It is said to have been an overnight stopping-off post for horses and carts during the transit of mail from places like Peterborough. The connection with the delivery of Royal Mail was officially acknowledged in 1989, and the prestigious title of 'Royal' was added to the name following a formal consent letter from the Queen's secretary. This acknowledgement was arranged by the current owner, Mrs Stoker, and she is very proud of not only the title of the pub but also the history of the building. The current restaurant, bar and lounge areas were a much later addition to the structure and, having talked with Mrs Stoker and bar manager Jon at length about the paranormal activity in the pub, they confirmed that the strange occurrences have always taken place in the older, original parts of the building. Mrs Stoker's history with the building dates back to 1989, when she initially took ownership. Jon, who has been bar manager for quite a few years, resides in a flat above the pub.

There are quite a few old photographs around the building relating to the history and previous occupants and, having always been very fond of the pictures and wanting to preserve the history, Sue has kept the photographs on display in the pub and restaurant. One of the photographs shows a soldier. Very intrigued by it, Sue carried out some research and learned that his name was Michael Branton. Sadly, he had fallen in France during the First World War and the family have often wondered if some of the unusual occurrences could be attributed to the spirit of Michael. Keen to learn more myself about the level of paranormal activity there, I talked at length with the owners, concluding that my investigation team would meet up with the family and their close friends to carry out an investigation.

Testimonies of Paranormal Activity

The earliest incident of paranormal activity that Sue was able to recall involved her daughter Lucy, who was aged about seven at the time. The pub was closed and Lucy was enjoying a game of pool with her dad when she suddenly paused, staring at the bar. Her dad asked her what was wrong and she replied, 'Daddy, I have just seen something very strange.' Upon further

Picture of First World War Soldier Michael Branton, believed to be one of the resident spirits at the pub. (Courtesy of Sue Stoker)

Royal Mail Cart. (Courtesy of Sue Stoker)

Bar where a bottle was thrown by an unknown entity. (Author's collection)

questioning, it transpired that she had seen a gentleman behind the bar, who had taken a bottle of beer and walked away holding it. The man was not known to her but she described him as looking like 'Benny from *Crossroads*', because he was wearing a similar hat. Since then, many other events have occurred and these can be summarised as follows:

- A bottle of tonic flew off the shelf and across the bar – the neck of the bottle was broken clean off and a member of staff had to duck to avoid being hit by it.
- Beer mugs that hang in the bar swing on their own.
- Two different chefs have experienced a rush of cold air in the kitchen.
- A 'presence' has been felt in the kitchen.

- There is sometimes a feeling of being watched, cold air with no source, and scratching sounds in a bedroom. (Upstairs flat)
- Hi-fi volume has been turned down several times. (Upstairs flat)
- TV channels have changed on their own. (Upstairs flat)
- Disembodied whistling has been heard coming from an empty bedroom. (Upstairs flat)
- A pile of plates in the kitchen was knocked onto the floor when no one was in there.
- A ship's bell behind the bar rings on its own.
- Set out cutlery has been messed up.
- A glass that had been thrown away many times kept reappearing on a shelf.

✖ A bin 'flew' across the room in the gentlemen's toilets as though it had been kicked.

The Investigation

The investigation consisted of a séance and also vigils in most rooms; EMF and EVP work was undertaken in those rooms and many photographs were taken.

During the vigil in the upstairs flat (occupied by Jon) Jon told us about a very close friend of his, who had tragically been killed in a car accident some years before. Jon had been devastated by this and, given that they had been so close, he has always kept a picture of them together on a unit above the stereo in his front room. Whilst we were taking about this, the EMF detector started to light up vigorously and, when holding it next to the photograph of Jon and his late best friend, it continued to do so. I moved the photograph onto the table in the centre of the room, where there were no sources of power that could set off the EMF detector, and held it next to the picture again – we were stunned to see it continue to light up and flicker right up to red. When I moved the KII from the picture, the lights all went out – but came straight back on again as soon as I put it back on the picture. In all of the investigations where I have been present, this is the most unusual EMF activity that I have seen. In addition to this, Jon spoke to his friend, asking if it was him lighting up the machine. Every time Jon spoke the machine would light up, seemingly in response.

Other areas of random electromagnetic energy were the bedroom (specifically Jon's bed) and the hallway outside the front room. Incidentally, whilst I was in the hallway with another team member, trying to find a source for the vigorous activity on the

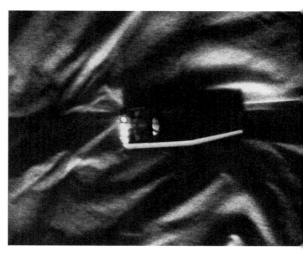

EMF detector lighting up Jon's bed. (Author's collection)

KII, I said, 'So there's no explanation for it lighting up over here then.' When reviewing the EVP audio after the investigation, I was very amused to hear a disembodied male voice saying, 'Yes there is!'

EVP Evidence

There were actually quite a few disembodied voices recorded during the investigation at the Royal Mail Cart:

'Are you standing in the hall?' … 'I'm right here.'
'Can you make a noise?' … 'Yes.'
'Is it a nice place?' (referring to where the spirits are now) … 'Yes.'
'I'd love to see you in my pictures.' … 'I'd love them.'
(Random male voice) 'I've just been to Stamford.'
(Spirit of Michael moving glass in séance) 'It's stuck, help please.'
(During séance) 'Jack, are you still there?' (Jack was Sue's father) … Yes.'
(During vigil) 'Can you knock twice?' … 'No.'

Séance. (Author's collection)

The sound of a dog barking was also recorded – which could explain some of the scratching sounds that had been reported in Jon's flat.

Following the vigil in the flat, we held a séance downstairs in the bar area. Quite early in the séance, the glass glided across the board towards Jon. There was a spirit wanting to connect with him who, when questioned for his name, confirmed the identity of Jon's best friend. In order to prove for Jon that it was really him we were speaking to, we asked when he had passed into spirit; he responded by confirming the year for us. He then wrote BED. When questioned, he said he was trying to tell Jon that it was him sitting on the bed earlier, lighting up the EMF detector. He also confirmed that it is him playing with the stereo, turning it down. Apparently, when he was alive there

was banter between the friends about the fact they didn't share the same taste in music, so this was quite humorous for Jon.

During the séance, a gentleman called Michael came to talk to us on the board. He began by telling us that it is his picture hanging in the restaurant. In response to our questions, he told us that he resided at the pub for seven years and he had indeed fallen in France during the First World War at the age of twenty-four. He had been married at the time and had three children. He told us the name of his wife, and that one of his daughters had been named after her. Around this time, a lady came on the board to talk to us and she gave her name as Ada – it is not clear whether she was connected to Michael but she confirmed herself to be a happy spirit connected with the pub, who likes to play tricks on people.

Some other experiences were noted during the investigation vigils:

- ☠ Several people felt a cold chill and goosebumps.
- ☠ A broom fell against the kitchen door – no one was touching it.
- ☠ A noise resembling a lit gas burner was heard in the kitchen, but stopped when people began talking about it.
- ☠ A piano was heard playing briefly in the lounge/bar area.
- ☠ Random cold spots were found with the thermometers.

Conclusion

From the paranormal activity, investigation and séance, it is clear that the Royal Mail Cart has several spirit visitors and residents, whose presence will always be welcomed by Sue and Jon, given their passion for preserving and celebrating the history of the pub. For Jon in particular the investigation was immensely enlightening, and he has taken much comfort from the possibility that his late best friend has never left his side.

Woodlands Hotel, Pinchbeck Road

Constructed in the early 1900s, this former residential property was transformed in the mid-1980s into an extremely elegant and beautiful hotel. It has been extended during its time as a hotel, but the building still retains many of its original Edwardian features.

Woodlands Hotel. (Author's collection)

The landing where 'Joyce' is said to spend much of her time, and the stairs that she has been seen descending. (Author's collection)

I learned on a visit to the hotel that the housekeepers – one of whom had been employed in her role for twenty-four years – had experienced some strange occurrences whilst going about their daily routine, so I interviewed them to find out more.

Upon meeting them, they opened the conversation by saying 'Her name is Joyce', with an affectionate laugh. The truth of the matter is they do not know her real name but have come to accept over the years that there is definitely a ghost in the hotel. They believe it to be a lady who, it is suspected, died many years ago in what is now Room 2

of the building. I asked about the activity they had experienced and they told me an interesting and quite humorous story about a gentleman who had stayed in Room 4. Apparently, his wife telephoned the room one morning during his stay, some time before 9 a.m. He had already gone to work but a mysterious woman had answered the phone. It is not known what was said during this conversation but his wife telephoned again later, managing to reach him this time. Somewhat distressed, she said, 'Who is staying in the room with you?' The staff at the hotel were able to confirm that no one was staying in the room with the gentleman and no one would have been in the room at that particular time. The housekeepers had not even arrived for their shift by then, so they had not been in the room either. The hotel owner at that time spoke to the gentleman's wife to offer reassurance, explaining that the hotel has a ghost and many unexplainable events are attributed to her. This is a very unusual story and I can't help but wonder how the gentleman explained himself upon going home. I can only hope his wife had an open mind! Many staff who have worked at Woodlands over the years have been required to stay overnight as part of their shift; most have refused to stay in Room 4, following reports that a 'lady' has walked through the room in the middle of the night. Staff have even opted to sleep downstairs on a sofa, rather than sleep in that particular room!

The activity at Woodlands Hotel is by no means restricted to the bedrooms. The current owner explained to me that sometimes when he is upstairs very late at night he will hear voices downstairs in the bar – but when he goes downstairs there is no one there. Another strange and quite frightening occurrence involved a Polish resident who stayed there regularly; he did not sleep well at night and often used to sit outside the front of the building. Very late on one particular night he was startled and then petrified when the figure of a woman, dressed in white, hurriedly 'swooped' past him and round the side of the building. In that instant he had wanted to call the police because he thought it was an intruder, but when he tried to give chase the woman had completely vanished. The staff said that he was left very pale and shaken by the experience.

The housekeepers have never actually seen Joyce but they describe her as a joker because things often disappear and reappear elsewhere, and she also turns the televisions on in the rooms. The most active rooms are Rooms 1-5, situated in the old part of the building, but the majority of the activity seems to take place in Room 4. Throughout the course of researching this book, I was approached by people wanting to share their stories and experiences of paranormal activity. One lady told me that she used to work at Woodlands Hotel and, again, named Room 4 as the most active of the haunted rooms – it's always exciting as an investigator when you find consistencies in several independent testimonies. She also informed me that she had once heard the sound of a piano playing in the bar area. Since there was no piano nearby, or any source for the sound, she found it bizarre. Apparently, Joyce doesn't venture into the new part of the building.

In the upper hall there used to be a large open landing, which was reduced to extend the room space. It is said that Joyce spends most of her time on the landing area and was actually seen gliding down the stairs by the previous owner of the hotel.

Whilst on my tour of the building, I had an unusual experience myself: I was chatting with one of the housekeepers in the small hallway outside the bedrooms and, simultaneously, we both reacted to seeing movement out in the landing through the small rectangular window in the door. It was as though someone had quickly passed us. I opened the door out into the landing and looked around – but there was no one nearby at all … could this have been Joyce making her presence felt? If it was, I wish she had stayed longer and introduced herself!

Whilst researching the hotel, it transpired that there was, in fact, once someone named Joyce residing at Woodlands; she apparently grew up there many years ago. It is somewhat coincidental that the female ghost was given the name Joyce by staff who had no knowledge of the Joyce who once lived there.

Elsom Cross Printers

Elsom Cross Printers opened on London Road, Spalding, as a family-run business in approximately 1957. For some time after, the Elsom family's home was located above the shop. Prior to this, the property had been unoccupied for several years following a tragic death on the premises. During the time that the Elsoms resided there, they developed a strong sense that they were not alone.

Cliff Elsom lived at the property until the age of seven, and had a playroom located on the third floor. The oppressive atmosphere in the playroom made him feel very uneasy and, whilst he personally never saw anything, he knew that something wasn't quite right. During that time, his sister also felt uncomfortable in the playroom. She further recalled that, on one occasion, she was followed down the stairs from the second floor to the first floor by a 'figure'.

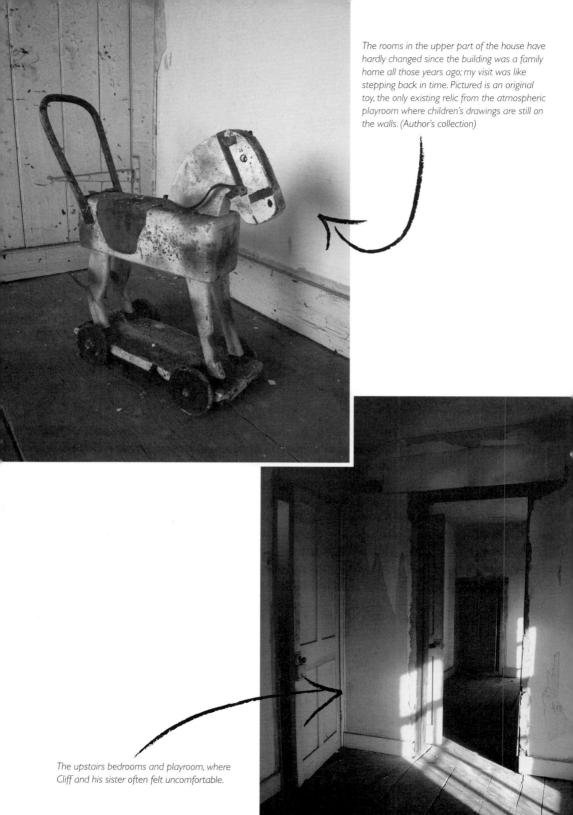

The rooms in the upper part of the house have hardly changed since the building was a family home all those years ago; my visit was like stepping back in time. Pictured is an original toy, the only existing relic from the atmospheric playroom where children's drawings are still on the walls. (Author's collection)

The upstairs bedrooms and playroom, where Cliff and his sister often felt uncomfortable.

Cliff also recalled that quite often, when his father Charlie went to the pub next door (then called the Bell), his mother would hear the sound of footsteps coming up the stairs into her bedroom. Initially she would think that her husband had come home, but would then realise that no one was there. This alone made her feel very anxious, but the next part was even worse. She would feel a cold sensation pressing against her face and, not knowing what to do, she would just keep her eyes closed and wait for the unpleasant and eerie feeling to stop.

When the Elsom family moved house, their printing business (still based in the building) continued to flourish. They eventually went into partnership with Geoff Hemsil, who worked in the building for fifty years. He recalled that when he was approximately seventeen years old, he had a strange experience while at work on the ground floor. One evening, at around 6 p.m., he was in the building completely by himself in the back room when he heard the sound of someone coming down the stairs to where he was standing. The footsteps were so heavy that he was sure there was an intruder in the building. Picking up a large printer's mallet, he nervously prepared to tackle the intruder. However, no

Elsom Cross Printers.

one appeared at the bottom of the stairs and, upon checking, no one was there, or even in the building. This experience left him feeling quite unnerved.

The office of Elsom Cross Printers is currently run by Jane Martin and she has confirmed that she has not had any unusual experiences in the building ... so far!

3

Bridge Street and the Priory

THE next few locations are in an area of Spalding that, many years ago, was the site of a large priory. There have been several reports of paranormal activity in this part of the town and it is highly possible that influences of the priory's past are causing the activity being reported today.

Monastic records show that the Spalding Priory was formed sometime between 1086 and 1090, when consent was formerly granted by William the Conqueror. There is no exact map on record of how it looked – the place was destroyed before official records began – but a plan was drawn up in 1666 showing how it was likely to have been set up (based on the typical layout of a Benedictine monastery). It is also unknown exactly where the church was within the monastery, as when it was destroyed in 1539 the stone was used to build houses in the town. However, based on the traditional layout of a monastery, and the location of the only existing remains of the Spalding Priory (Abbey Buildings on Priory Road), it is likely that the church was located on what is now Vine Street car park. The adjacent cemetery would have been located between Vine Street and Bridge Street. It is noteworthy that during recent renovation

work in what is now Santander on Bridge Street, a number of human skeletons and skulls were excavated from beneath the floor. There are said to be many more human remains underneath the shops along Bridge Street.

In addition to a cemetery once eerily being situated in that part of the town, there are certain events that could have led to the existence of restless spirits in this area. At that time, priests were not meant to marry but could have as many mistresses

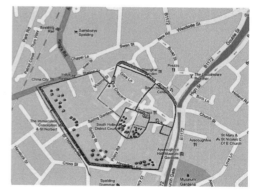

Author's interpretation of where the Spalding Priory was situated. It is believed that the monks would fetch their drinking water from the river Westlode, which flowed along what is now Westlode Street and New Road. (Courtesy of Google Maps ©2011 Google-Map Data © 2011 Tele Atlas)

as they wished. However, an Act was passed in 1225 which meant that the concubines of priests would be refused burial on consecrated ground and would therefore have been buried outside the parameters of the cemetery. Furthermore, there was a tragic incident just after the dissolution of the monastery, at a time when the buildings were falling into disrepair. They were used as a meeting place for parties; at one particular birthday party people had become rowdy, jumping up and down and dancing on the upper floor. The floor subsequently gave way, killing not only those who fell, but many other people whom they landed on and crushed.

There are several accounts of paranormal activity in the area of the old priory and Bridge Street. We begin within the walls of Abbey Buildings – now split into a terrace of houses.

Abbey Buildings, Priory Road

Local historians are confident that Abbey Buildings once served as the prior's lodgings, given that there are two very large original fireplaces within the buildings. Whilst out on my travels, I was approached by a lady who currently resides in one of the houses within the Abbey Buildings. When she learned of my interest in the paranormal, and my investigation work, she was very keen for me to visit her home.

Abbey Buildings, Priory Road: the only priory buildings still standing. Whilst now converted for practical living, there has been little change to the structure inside and out from all those centuries ago. As such, they have retained spectacular character and atmosphere. (Author's collection)

Priory Road, with the former Johnson Hospital visible on the right. (Author's collection)

Bridge Street. (Author's collection)

Upon entering the house I was immediately in awe of its beauty and character. Even inside, the original fabric of the building remains seemingly unchanged from its monastery days; it is very atmospheric. The first unusual event recalled by the current resident was when she came downstairs one morning to find that a banana stand, complete with bananas, had been placed in the middle of the kitchen floor during the night. She was baffled by this because it obviously hadn't fallen – the bananas were all intact on the upright stand and the stand

itself had a ceramic base, which would have broken had it fallen.

She also recalled that she had been unable to sleep one night when she was downstairs in the lounge area – a room which she describes as 'creepy', as she often feels as though she is not alone there. She confessed that she could not turn off the light that night because the oppressive atmosphere was overwhelming.

The other incident she remembered was an experience that her room-mate had in one of the bedrooms. One night, when she was half-asleep in bed, she felt as though a spider was crawling on her – and she woke up to the sight of a hand on her shoulder. Just as quickly, it disappeared. Could this be the presence of a monk or another soul connected to the Spalding Priory?

A figure of a man has been seen on several occasions walking down the middle of Priory Road during the night, in front of the old Johnson Hospital. The figure mysteriously vanishes within seconds of being seen.

💀💀💀

Bridge Street is only a small street in Spalding town centre. However, several shops and former private residences along this stretch have experienced paranormal activity over the years – and some still do.

Morris & Mennie Estate Agents

Staff at Morris & Mennie have reported that when they are downstairs they can hear footsteps upstairs, as though someone else is in the building. They have also each described sensing a presence when they are upstairs on their own, although they never actually see anything. Many of the shops along Bridge Street have a hatch in the floor, which reveals an underground cellar. I was fortunate enough to get a peek inside the one at Morris & Mennie. The cellars are very eerie inside, some having remains of fireplaces and large living spaces. You can also see the original steps that would have taken residents out onto the streets of Spalding in previous centuries.

Large cellar at Morris & Mennie. (Author's collection)

Inside Geoff Neal's dry-cleaning shop. (Author's collection)

Geoff Neal & Son Dry Cleaners

I spoke at length with Geoff about the paranormal activity he has experienced over the years in his shop, which has been based in Bridge Street since 1988. He explained to me that, whilst the strange disturbances mysteriously stopped about twelve years ago, he still feels uncomfortable talking about it and even thinking about it. He recalled that there was one specific paranormal event that he experienced roughly once every three months. It would begin with a chilling draught, seemingly from nowhere, which would travel down the stairs and all the way through the shop. At the same time, a panel that protrudes from the ceiling would violently shake for a minute or so. Geoff described feeling chills and goosebumps throughout the experience, and all the hairs on his arms would stand on end.

In addition to the unexplainable draught and shaking of the ceiling panel, he also recalled several occasions when a wooden door to a very small room at the top of the building would mysteriously unbolt and open itself. The room is so small that Geoff feels it is likely to have been occupied by a child in the eighteenth century, when the building would have been a family home. It was clear from talking with Geoff that he was always a little shaken by the paranormal activity, and was very glad when it stopped. I wish him well and really hope that he does not have to experience any further activity of that nature.

The tiny door in Geoff Neal's building that has unbolted, unlatched and opened on its own. (Author's collection)

M&Co.

I spoke to the manager of M&Co. about some of the strange things she has experienced at the clothing store in her twenty

The staff door at the back of M&Co. that opens and closes on its own. (Author's collection)

staff often hear the sound of people upstairs talking and running around, though upon investigation they always find it is completely empty up there.

Furthermore, there are occasions now when, sitting in her office before opening up the shop, she will hear the sound of the heavy fire door opening and slamming shut. She has assumed it to be her assistant manager entering the building, but upon investigation she has found the building deserted, and the assistant manager has arrived at work several minutes later. There were some weeks when this would happen almost every day and the manager was so baffled by it that she even checked the door was not defective. One particular day, the assistant manager arrived for work early and both of them experienced the strange phenomenon of the door opening and closing by itself. Having been unable to find an explanation for this, the manager was somewhat relieved that it had now been witnessed by someone else too.

The incidents that occur are by no means frequent, and the staff can go for long periods of time without experiencing anything at all. During my interview with the staff of M&Co., they were adamant that there is never anything negative about the strange events – in fact, they sense that they are protected by whoever it is that is sharing their space, and the overall energy feels very positive.

years of working in the building. She began by telling me that on many occasions when she has opened the store in the morning, she has found random items in the middle of the floor that had not been there the previous evening upon locking up. Also, the

4

Ayscoughfee Hall Museum

WHEN it comes to reputedly haunted buildings in Spalding, few are more talked about than Ayscoughfee Hall, where local folklore tells of a White Lady that walks the floors of this ancient and picturesque manor house. In 2010, my curiosity about the ghostly White Lady led to SPI (Spalding Paranormal Investigations) being the first ever paranormal group invited into the hall, in an attempt to establish whether there really are spirits present at Ayscoughfee or whether it is mere urban legend.

I researched right back to the beginnings of Ayscoughfee Hall, looking at its construction, alterations over the years and, perhaps most importantly, previous occupants – after all, I wanted to find out who the mysterious White Lady could be. The earliest record of a building on the site is in the 1086 Domesday Book, but the original Ayscoughfee manor house was built in the 1450s in one building campaign. The roof timbers of the Great Hall and both north and south wings still survive, and have been dendrochronologically dated to 1451, i.e. the oak trees used were felled in 1451. It is not known who built Ayscoughfee Hall, although recent research suggests that

it was a member of the Ayscoughfee family. Local legend, though, states that a member of the Aldwyn family built Ayscoughfee, due to the reference to '… my grete place in Spalding' in Sir Nicholas Aldwyn's will (1499). It has long been held that this refers to Ayscoughfee Hall.

After a series of other owners, Maurice Johnson (I) took ownership of the estate in 1683, later passing it to his eldest son (also Maurice). Maurice Johnson (II), an antiquary, founded Spalding Gentlemen's Society in 1712, after establishing the slightly less formal literary society in Spalding a few years previously. Spalding Gentlemen's Society is still in existence, and has the second oldest museum in the UK (after the Ashmolean Museum in Oxford). It is recorded that Maurice (II) and his wife Elizabeth had approximately twenty-six children.

The Ayscoughfee estate remained in the Johnson family until 1851, when the Johnsons moved away from Spalding following the tragic death of their young daughter. Of all the owners of Ayscoughfee throughout the Johnson generations (1683-1851), there were six by the name of Maurice Johnson, some of whom instigated

Ayscoughfee Hall. (Author's collection)

significant alterations to the structure and layout of the building. When the Johnsons left Spalding, Ayscoughfee Hall was rented out on lease to various parties, before finally being sold to local citizens in 1898 by the last Johnson, Isabella, who was married to Maurice Johnson (VI). In accordance with contractual obligations connected with the sale, the new trustees were to use the building as a museum and recreational ground to benefit the residents of Spalding. Ownership was transferred to the Urban District Council in 1902, and Ayscoughfee School (a private education establishment) was opened on the upper floor in 1920, closing in 1982. In 1987, ownership of the building was transferred to South Holland District Council, and the current museum opened to the public.

Given the extensive history of Ayscoughfee, I felt that it would be very surprising to find nothing at all during a paranormal investigation. However, the history, interesting as it was, had not given me any obvious clue as to the identity of the White Lady. There were no traumatic or dramatic historical events that came to my attention in relation to a lady at Ayscoughfee, so none of the women that would have occupied the estate really stood out. Much of the history that I read placed emphasis on the gentlemen that once owned the building. This is to be expected, as the property would have been passed down through the male line and therefore women were not recorded or mentioned much in historical record.

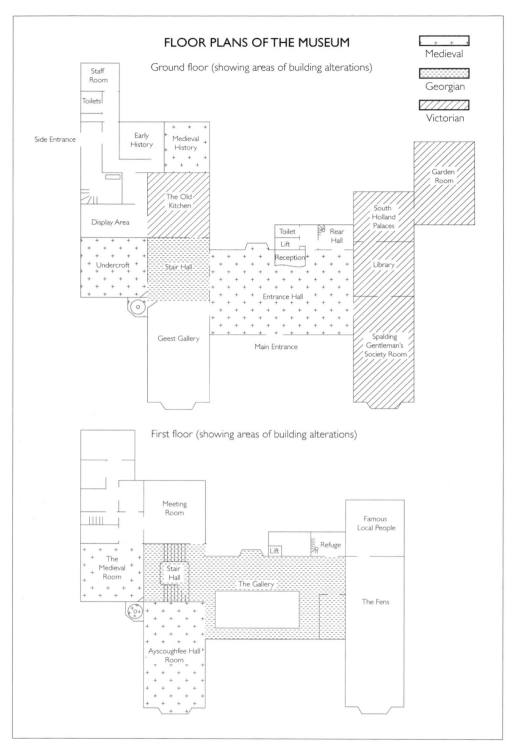

FLOOR PLANS OF THE MUSEUM

Medieval

Georgian

Victorian

Ground floor (showing areas of building alterations)

Staff Room

Toilets

Side Entrance

Early History

Medieval History

The Old Kitchen

Display Area

South Holland Palaces

Garden Room

Toilet

Lift

Reception

Rear Hall

Undercroft

Stair Hall

Library

Entrance Hall

Geest Gallery

Main Entrance

Spalding Gentleman's Society Room

First floor (showing areas of building alterations)

Meeting Room

Famous Local People

The Medieval Room

Stair Hall

Lift

Refuge

The Gallery

The Fens

Ayscoughfee Hall Room

Plans of the current layout, showing progressive alterations to the building. (Image courtesy of Ayscoughfee Hall)

In the weeks leading up to the investigation I made several visits to Ayscoughfee, familiarising myself with the layout of the building and speaking at length with the staff about their experiences there. I established that although no members of staff had seen a White Lady, or any other spirit presence, there is one particular corridor – located to the rear of the kitchen, where the toilets are situated – where some staff experience an oppressive and uncomfortable feeling.

The building has seen many alterations and I felt extremely privileged to be taken to explore original areas of the house that are, for practical and safety reasons, not open to the general public and remain out of view. The investigation to be carried out by SPI was to be conducted on an 'access all areas' basis, and it was therefore essential to familiarise ourselves with the whereabouts of every door, room and staircase, and the overall layout, so that we could structure the team to cover the whole building thoroughly. The stone spiral staircase leading up to the Tower Bedroom was extremely spectacular; I felt like Rapunzel standing in that room, admiring the view of the flowers below!

The Investigation

Following much preparation, on the evening of Friday, 17 September 2010, the Spalding Paranormal Investigations team, together with representatives from South Holland District Council and the Lincolnshire Free Press, all gathered on site. There was much excitement and anticipation surrounding the investigation night, as we were all so privileged to be involved.

Some of the investigation team and guests. Left to right: Stuart Moulder, Pam Stretton, Gemma King, Phil King, Vicky Thomson, Councillor Howard Johnson. (Courtesy of John Baker)

The corridor to the rear of the kitchen, where staff have sometimes felt uneasy. This whole section of the building was added in the Victorian era. It is believed that the medieval kitchen would have been sited roughly where the Garden Room now stands. Prior to that, it is likely to have been in a separate structure, in order to mitigate the risk of fire.

Spiral staircase leading up to the remote Tower Bedroom. (Author's collection)

Furthermore, given that this was uncharted territory, the team had no idea what to expect in the way of activity. Naturally, every investigation is different, but often you have a preconceived idea of how active a place is – and we had no clue in relation to Ayscoughfee. This made it very exciting indeed.

In order to cover the whole building thoroughly and minimise noise contamination, it was decided that we should split the group into two teams. We divided the building into zones so that each team would spend a fixed amount of time in one area before moving on to the next. Organising the teams and managing the time in this way meant that each individual room would be covered twice; we would have the potential to capture more evidence and there would be fewer feet clomping through the building on the audio recordings. On reflection, this was definitely the best way to conduct the investigation as parts of the building are very prone to echoing. In such an environment, it is best to have fewer people present and little or no movement. It is also advisable to stay close to the voice recorder when you are speaking, so sound can be picked up clearly.

When the equipment had been set up, the base readings were taken in accordance with our usual investigation procedures. During this process, the investigators picked up high EMF readings in the 'oppressive corridor' to the rear of the kitchen and also experienced the hairs on their arms standing on end.

Often on investigations where teams are split, the groups will have different experiences when investigating the same area respectively, and areas that are seemingly inactive to one team can be quite eventful for the other; this was definitely the case

The Library, active for Team 2 during the investigation. (Author's collection)

with Ayscoughfee Hall. For example, Team 1 found the Gallery to be very active, but it was quiet and pretty uneventful during the vigil carried out by Team 2. On the flipside, Team 2 had notable experiences in the Library, where Team 1 found the Library quite flat in terms of activity.

Here is a summary of events that were encountered during the investigation:

Library and Great Hall

During the vigil in these areas, team member Stuart invited any spirits present to light up the EMF detector, which was placed on the desk. The machine lit up more than once on cue. When the resident spirits were invited to make a noise to confirm their presence, tapping was heard – on the desk itself. We asked them to do it again for validation and immediately heard a further tap, also on the desk.

Large orb anomaly pictured on the kitchen step during the investigation; nothing was visible to the team, although we were aware of the high EMF readings at the time. The bright flash on my camera lit up the room in this photograph! (Author's collection)

Moving orb anomaly captured on camera in the corridor to the rear of the kitchen. (Author's collection)

There were many large white orb anomalies picked up in the photographs from this area. When I invited the resident spirits to stand with Vicky for a photograph, several appeared at ground level close to where she was standing.

Kitchen and Rear Corridor

When my team was investigating in the kitchen area, inviting spirits to move or bang something to show their presence, I was slightly worried about the beautiful china on the dresser at the back of the room. However, there were no banging noises recorded by either team in this area. That said, there were very strong EMF readings recorded in the kitchen itself and in the adjacent 'oppressive corridor'. One particular EMF reading in the corridor seemed to take the shape of a person and was completely remote. When the machine was pulled away from the remote spot, the lights went green; when placed back into the spot, the machine lit up red again. Photographs in this area also produced some strange orb anomalies, one of which seemed to be moving extremely quickly at the time the picture was taken.

Meeting Room (probable former chapel)

We did not expect to experience much in the way of activity here, given that during the day it is frequently occupied by staff and they have never encountered anything unusual. However, despite its humble appearance, it was actually one of the most eventful rooms on the night of the investigation. As Team 1 sat around the desk with the lights out during their vigil, a laptop switched itself on and, moments later, the EMF meter lit

Meeting Room. It is speculated that the chapel, consecrated in 1486, was located in this room. It has also been suggested that the exposed brickwork to the left of the mirror might have been where holy water was kept. (Author's collection)

up vigorously, all the way to red. Team 2 also experienced strange activity in this room. When the spirits were invited to light up the EMF meter, it lit up all the way to red on several occasions. Furthermore, whilst lighting up, it inexplicably fell off the saucer that it was perched on. We did explore the possibility that a vibration from the flickering lights may have caused the machine to fall – but we quickly dismissed this, reaching the conclusion that the machines do not vibrate at all when the lights go off. Furthermore, it would have taken a strong force to knock it over. This event was captured on film.

The Gallery

Although inactive for Team 2, Team 1 experienced remote temperature drops in the Gallery when inviting any resident spirits to interact with them. Seemingly on cue, the temperature in one remote spot dropped by several degrees.

Early History Room

The most significant event that occurred in this room was that the gentleman from the press, John Baker, was taken ill. He started to feel cold, uncomfortable and nauseous. He confirmed that the feeling immediately evaporated upon leaving this room. Interestingly, this room is located next to the 'oppressive corridor'.

EVP Evidence

Reviewing the audio after an investigation is just as exciting for me as being at the investigation itself, because often when areas seem inactive on the night, the audio tells a different story. This was most definitely the case with Ayscoughfee and here are some of the EVP clips that were extracted from various rooms:

The Garden Room

This was one of the rooms where I least expected to capture evidence – it was a later addition to the building and seemed pretty quiet during the vigil. However, whilst snapping pictures on my camera, I explained the purpose of the gadgets to the spirit residents and invited them to appear in the pictures. Just a few seconds later, whilst I was still taking pictures, a gentleman's voice was recorded, saying 'Behind you!'

The Gallery. (Author's collection)

The Meeting Room being investigated by Team 1. (Picture courtesy of John Baker)

The Meeting Room

This was the location of the tea machine and, whilst in that room, Team 1 engaged in a brief conversation about how they like their tea and coffee. As everyone was chipping in to the debate, a very clear female voice said 'African tan'. This is most baffling, because the only woman in the room at the time was Pam and she did not say it – it was also abundantly clear from the audio that it was not her voice.

Medieval Room

This was, without doubt, the most eerie EVP captured on the investigation night. As Team 1 enter the Medieval Room, you can hear the clomp, clomp, clomp of shoes, then a gentleman's voice saying, 'Get out!'

No electronic voice phenomena were captured by Team 2 in this room.

The Kitchen

During the vigil in the kitchen, I asked, 'Is there someone that likes to walk around in the corridor? If that's you, could you tell us your name?' The voice recorder picked up a response, 'That's the cook.'

Conclusion

I will always recall my involvement with the Ayscoughfee Hall team with deep affection and much gratitude for the opportunity that they gave us. The investigation that I

The Kitchen. (Author's collection)

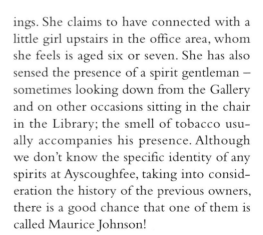

The last members of the Johnson family to reside at Ayscoughfee Hall: Maurice (VI) and his wife Isabella. (Courtesy of Ayscoughfee Hall)

was extremely humbled and privileged to be a part of will always stand out in my mind as the pinnacle of my investigating experiences.

Is Ayscoughfee Hall haunted? Whilst there were no ghostly sightings on the night of our investigation, the experiences of the team and the evidence captured does strongly suggest that there are spirit residents. Who are they? We don't know. But since the investigation, I have spoken with a spiritually gifted lady who frequently visits Ayscoughfee Hall for business meetings. She claims to have connected with a little girl upstairs in the office area, whom she feels is aged six or seven. She has also sensed the presence of a spirit gentleman – sometimes looking down from the Gallery and on other occasions sitting in the chair in the Library; the smell of tobacco usually accompanies his presence. Although we don't know the specific identity of any spirits at Ayscoughfee, taking into consideration the history of the previous owners, there is a good chance that one of them is called Maurice Johnson!

5

The Horrific Ordeal of a Spalding Family

FOLLOWING the local publicity surrounding SPI's investigation of Ayscoughfee Hall, I was approached by a lady who had, over time, become quite distressed as a result of an ongoing problem in her home that had been adversely affecting her whole family. She asked if my team could help her to investigate, with a view to resolving it. Given the sensitive nature of this particular case, I feel that the family is extremely brave in allowing me to tell their story. I don't feel it appropriate to discuss their identity or specific location in Spalding, and have therefore agreed with the family that their real names will not be used.

Their story begins in a modern semi-detached home where a mother resides with her two teenage daughters. The mother, whom I will refer to as Julia, was the first to experience a disturbance. It occurred one night when she was in bed, drifting off to sleep. Her bedroom door had remained shut but she had suddenly become aware of a significant weight pressing down on the bed, as though someone was sitting on it, and at this time she felt an oppressive presence in the room. She was wide awake by now and facing away from whatever it was.

She took the decision not to look, because she strongly felt that if she turned around she would see something that she did not want to see. Instead, she pulled the quilt up around her face as far as it would go and waited for the mysterious presence to leave. Moments later, she felt the compressed bed rise up again, as whatever it was seemed to silently get up. Julia did not see it leave but felt the oppressive feeling disappear. She did not talk about this experience with her daughters as she did not want to frighten them. However, a few days later, she noticed further activity. Upon going downstairs one morning, she discovered that an ornamental pot in the living room, usually kept on the hearth, had found its way onto the carpet – over 1ft away from where it had been. She asked her daughters if either of them had moved it and neither of them knew anything about it. Little did they know that this was only the start of what was to be a very difficult and unpleasant year, where they would become plagued by activity from a very persistent – and at times scary – spirit.

Further unusual events were soon noted by the eldest daughter, Melody, who started to hear strange sounds in the mornings whilst getting ready to leave the house.

Melody was always the last person to leave in the morning, but whilst in her upstairs bedroom she would frequently hear noises downstairs. On one particular morning, she was up in her bedroom straightening her hair when, from just outside her doorway on the landing, she could hear a disturbing and frightening sound, which she identified as a 'man groaning'. Not knowing what to think or do – and in a state of shock from what she was hearing – she literally froze with fear for a few moments. She then hurriedly gathered her belongings together and left the house. Melody told me that whilst it was clearly a man's voice that she could hear, she could not decipher any actual words amidst the groaning, but added that it did not sound like he was in pain.

On another occasion, she was lying in bed at night, having just turned out her light, when she heard one of the drawers in her nearby unit close. At around this time, she had also begun to see shadows and mists travelling up the stairs in the house, sometimes hovering at the top. This was also experienced by her younger sister Suzie, who started waking up in the night to find a shadowy figure leaning over her bed. Suzie would also feel someone touching her, and things were being moved about on her dressing table.

One of the most frightening experiences for Suzie occurred when she was sitting on her bed doing some homework. Her bedroom is only a small room and, on the day in question, the bedroom door (which opens right next to her) was open. As she was working, a man's hand suddenly reached inside the door, picked up a piece of paper from the unit just inside the room and threw it onto the floor. All that Suzie saw was the hand and lower arm of this spirit. It promptly disappeared after doing this, leaving her very shaken.

The activity around the upstairs hall and in the girls' rooms was causing a lot of distress to the family – to the point where Suzie, at times, was too afraid to sleep in the house. This was the stage when SPI became involved.

As part of the investigation, we held a séance in the home to establish the identity of the troublesome spirit. Following some pleasant messages from spirit relatives of the family, we were contacted by a gentleman who gave his name as Cedrick. He told us that it was him causing the disturbances. We asked if he realised that he was scaring the girls and he said 'No', then spelled 'Sorry'. In an attempt to bring closure to the situation, we asked him what he wanted. Sometimes spirits are trying to get our attention for a particular reason – on previous investigations, we have found that spirits have been grounded (unable to move on) and we have been able to resolve the problem. Unfortunately, in this case the spirit was not in need of help and merely told us that he wanted 'Suzie'. We told him that he was frightening the family, did not belong in the house, and that he had to leave. He did not respond to this request but it was now clear that he had formed an attachment to the family – in particular to Suzie.

After our investigation, I told the family that if they experienced anything else they should assert their authority and tell the spirit out loud to leave. It is vital to reclaim your space in uncomfortable situations like this, where an unwanted entity seems to be manifesting, and in many cases it can make it go away. It is said that, as with poltergeists, troublesome spirits prey on the vulnerable, drawing on negative energy created by stressful situations. Victims of this kind of activity therefore need to stay strong and assertive.

A few days went by and the activity started up again. The mist became visible at the top of the stairs and sometimes in mirrors. In addition to this, the family's sleep was frequently being disturbed. Then, one morning, Melody was alone in her bedroom when she became aware of noises downstairs. She could hear cupboards and drawers in the kitchen opening and closing and this really frightened her, to the point where she had to call her grandad from her mobile phone, asking him to come round and get her. She was too frightened to open her bedroom door and go downstairs.

Given the length of time that this relentless activity had been going on, the family were now at their wits' end. Being of Christian faith, Julia had previously approached her local parish about the problem. However, the priest there had been reluctant to become involved in the situation – and now she did not know what to do, feeling that she had tried everything and there was no solution. I was very frustrated for this family. We had now become quite close as friends and the continuing activity that they were experiencing was clearly causing a lot of distress and anxiety. It literally seemed to take over their home and their lives.

We became aware of a Roman Catholic priest whom we were told might be able to assist the family. I telephoned him as soon as I could to explain what had happened to date and to ask for his help and guidance. He was very compassionate and understanding, telling me that he had assisted in many similar cases before. He agreed to attend the home that evening.

The family took some much-needed comfort, reassurance and renewed hope from the priest's initial visit, for this was to be the beginning of a process that they hoped would expel the unwanted energy

This picture was taken by accident on Melody's phone when she was gathering her belongings to go out one evening. It shows a distorted image of Suzie's room and a strange dark shape which we believe to be a spirit gentleman, dressed in black, perched on the edge of the bed to the right of the chest of drawers. No image was visible to her in the room at the time it was taken. (Courtesy of Melody)

from their lives. Prayers were said in every room of the house and a cross was marked on each of the floors in holy water. The priest also left a bottle of holy water with the family for their protection. In addition to this, he left his phone number and said that they could call him at any time of the day or night if they needed help. This was immensely comforting for the family who, following the priest's visit, felt much more positive about the prospect of finally being able to move on from what had been a very difficult year.

After this, the activity seemed to calm down significantly, although it never completely ceased. One day, Melody was about to have a bath when there was a knock on the bathroom door. The door was slightly ajar and the knock was enough to move it further open. Upon opening the door, it was clear that there was no one there, and Suzie and Julia were downstairs, nowhere near the bathroom. Another thing that Melody found disturbing was that she had received a special glass ornament for her birthday and had put it on top of the mantelpiece with all her birthday cards, only to find it smashed to pieces on the floor the following day. It had been very carefully positioned and no one in her family had been near it. There were no windows open or draughts, and there was no way for the ornament to fall down on its own. A picture had also fallen from the mantelpiece on a different occasion.

Suzie was still having strange experiences too – such as seeing the shadowy figure in her bedroom, seeing a mist in the corner of the room, and sometimes enduring the feeling of being touched. On one occasion, she was alone in the house, sitting on the living-room floor doing some homework, when a tealight candle which was on top of the television suddenly started to move to the left, completely on its own, in a gradual shuffle. Then, in one big whooshing movement, it flew off the end of the television and onto the floor in front of her, leaving Suzie extremely frightened.

After a few weeks of escalating activity, the family decided to call upon the priest again. He attended the property and recited further prayers, again using the holy water to mark a cross in every room. Sadly, as with the previous visit, it did not result in the activity stopping, although it did calm down for a short period. When the activity heightened again, the priest took the decision to intensify his approach and he invited four other priests to join him at the property, where they spent several hours holding Mass in the front room and saying prayers around the home. Unfortunately, as the disturbances continued in the following weeks, it was clear that very drastic action was needed to rid the home of the problem. In view of this, the priest decided to arrange an exorcism of both the house and the family.

There is only one Roman Catholic priest in the Lincolnshire area qualified to carry out an exorcism, and arrangements were made for him to attend the property as soon as possible. The exorcism began with an opening prayer and this was followed by the Ritual of Exorcism. The ritual itself has several different parts, consisting of prayers, psalms, scripture, and various commands. Holy water was also used on the family to cast out demonic entities.

Whilst stories like this family's do frequently occur, exorcisms are quite rare and are generally a last resort – the final stage in a long, gruelling process where it is clear that the problem cannot be eliminated by any other means. Often it can take many weeks to completely eliminate the problem. Following the exorcism in this case, the activity around the house has calmed significantly, which is good news for the family. That said, it is not a completely happy ending for the youngest daughter, Suzie.

Suzie's sensitivity to spirits is thought to date back to around the age of nine, when she used to 'see faces', which she would then draw. She also used to report being visited by other children while in bed. Very recently, following the exorcism, she was in bed trying to sleep when she became aware of someone shouting in her ear. It was a little boy shouting out his name. She started to feel his face up against hers. She acknowledged the name by shouting it back – almost like a reflex response – but felt very uncomfortable during the experience. She still reports being touched by people and seeing shadows.

Moreover, at the time of the disturbances, not all of Suzie's experiences were taking place in the home. She recalled walking to school one day and seeing an elderly woman coming towards her with a dog. She looked up and the pair exchanged 'Good Mornings' as they passed each other, but then, as she looked behind her, the woman and dog had gone – completely vanished – and there was nowhere they could have gone.

Whilst many people would see this as a 'gift', Suzie doesn't want it, doesn't like to talk about it and wishes it would stop happening. Suzie's mother Julia told me that when she herself was a young child, her house was haunted by a monk, and amidst all the activity that would take place she used to communicate with him personally. She would tap out a rhythm on the window sill and he would tap it back to her. The fact that the family are all quite sensitive to spirits could be the reason I was unable to capture any actual evidence of paranormal activity with my camera or audio devices – because some of the activity is seemingly only visible or audible to them. Of course, there is still the physical activity of cupboards and drawers closing on their own, ornaments smashing, objects being moved and paper being thrown on the floor and, whilst I was unable to capture any evidence of the paranormal activity myself in this case, I believe that the picture inadvertently taken on Melody's phone is clear evidence of the perpetrator.

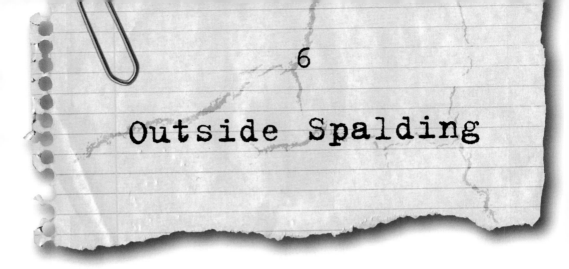

Outside Spalding

The Chequers Hotel, High Street, Holbeach

This hotel is situated opposite All Saints' Church and was built in approximately 1660 by Adlard Stukeley, the father of William Stukeley (founder of the Society of Antiquaries). A hospital (erected in 1351) had previously stood on this site, and was used to care for poor parishioners. Whilst neglect and deterioration led to the gradual demise of the hospital, the Chequers Hotel still stands in its former seventeenth-century glory, having changed little in external appearance since its construction all those years ago.

Testimonies of Activity

I made contact with the hotel after being intrigued by the experiences of a former staff member. She described instances when she would cash up at approximately 1 a.m. and, whilst sitting in the upstairs office, would hear children running up and down the corridor outside the room. This would leave her totally 'freaked out'. She also described occasions when she would be doing the housekeeping in Room 6 and no matter how much she tidied one particular bed in there, it would have an imprint on it moments later, as though someone was sitting on it. She also said that a man who once stayed in this room reported that, while he was asleep during the night, an unknown force lay on top of him. Apparently, the sensation was so strong that his breathing became restricted; he appeared quite shaken by the experience when he reported it to staff the following morning. Many other residents have reported strange occurrences during their stay at the Chequers, but that particular gentleman's story stood out in her mind.

Another part of the building where she had experienced something unusual was the cellar. She recalled going down there on one occasion to fetch some alcopops and, while there, heard light-heeled footsteps approaching. Out of the corner of her eye she saw a figure walk past the entrance to the cellar. When she went back upstairs, moments later, it soon became apparent that there was no one else in that area of the building and her female boss was sitting at the bar, nowhere near the cellar entrance. This experience stayed with the member of staff and left her feeling very reluctant to enter the cellar on her own

THE CHEQUERS HOTEL

Above *The Chequers. (Author's collection)*

Right *The cellar, where a former member of staff heard ghostly footsteps and another member of staff caught a glimpse of a ghostly gentleman walking past. This picture shows one of the many former tunnels that ran beneath the town, now blocked off. This particular tunnel leads to the nearby cemetery. (Author's collection)*

again. Another report of paranormal activity had come from the housekeeper at that time, who heard a disembodied voice calling out her name.

As I concluded my interview, she stated that the two years she had spent working at the Chequers had completely changed her beliefs with regard to the paranormal. Prior to this time, she had been a total non-believer in the types of phenomena that she had since encountered.

The manager confirmed to me that unusual occurrences had been reported by both staff and residents. She invited me to meet her at the hotel, look around the building, and listen to the accounts of activity; naturally, I was very keen to oblige! At the time of writing, the manager has been working at the hotel for four years. The first unusual event she noticed was the gas in the cellar switching on and off, seemingly on its own. This would mostly occur during the night and she would discover the problem the following morning. The canister has a nozzle at the top that has to be physically turned off, and nobody could have done this after lock-up.

In addition to this, she told me that she resides in the flat attached to the hotel. The day she moved in, the previous owner (a great believer in all things paranormal and apparently sensitive to spirits) had said to her, 'Don't move the TV from where I put it because they don't like it.' Intrigued by this statement, she questioned it and was told that there was a playful little spirit boy resident, who liked to play in a particular area. Not taking too much notice of this advice, the manager put the television where she wanted it. Straightaway, unexplainable things started to happen. She was listening to her stereo whilst washing up and suddenly the music became louder – progressing from 20 on the dial to full blast – and she started to hear all kinds of strange bumps and thuds throughout the night. Remembering the advice that she had been given by the previous occupant, she acknowledged the presence of the playful little boy and asked him to stop – and has not had any problems since, although her dog frequently stares at empty space and barks at 'nothing'. This is the same advice I give to people who are encountering a level of activity that is making them feel uncomfortable; many spirits interact with us because they want to get our attention,

and often simply acknowledging their presence can be enough to calm the activity.

During my conversation with the manager, she confirmed that most of the activity at the hotel occurs upstairs. At this point, the hotel housekeeper gave me a tour of the building and the 'hotspots'. She had been a housekeeper there for two years and had experienced a lot during that time. The housekeeper spoke affectionately about the spirits in the hotel, adding that she often asks out loud for them to leave her alone to get on with her cleaning; for this reason, they do not tend to bother her.

She did recall one occasion, though, when she was upstairs ironing in a disused bar and a black-hooded figure 'whooshed' by her, seemingly floating above floor level. Trying to rationalise her experience, she checked that it was not a reflection of someone nearby, but there was no one around and she noted that a reflection would not have been possible given the route taken by the figure. Shaken by her experience, she went downstairs – but returned minutes later to try to make sense of it. Right at that moment, three optics (drink dispensers) flicked up, one after another. The housekeeper was scared by this experience but added that, other than this, she had never had a negative or frightening experience in the hotel. She described the vibe of the 'active' areas of the hotel, such as the corridor, as having a 'warm' feel about them; and I have to say, following my visit to the hotel, this was also my view.

Having toured each of the hotel rooms and listened to the housekeeper's experiences, the final part of my tour took me into the cellar. Having now heard all of the accounts of activity around the beautiful, historic and highly atmospheric building, I was in a position to summarise the strange events as follows:

The Cellar – Disembodied footsteps, a shadowy figure walking past the top of the steps, and the current owner experiencing an unknown entity tampering with the nozzle on the gas canister. Also, a male member of staff saw the legs and feet of a man (wearing black trousers and black shoes) walking past him in the cellar as he was bending down to collect bottles. The man appeared solid and footsteps were heard as he passed – but the staff member could not place the man as an employee and noticed that he vanished, when there was nowhere he could have gone.

Upstairs bar – Dark-hooded figure seen gliding across the room and tampering with optics on the bar.

Upstairs corridor – Generally playful, disembodied sounds of children running about and giggling.

Room 5 – Where the housekeeper feels the most uncomfortable. An unexplained fire occurred in this room many years ago when a heater was mysteriously turned on and malfunctioned, setting the curtains alight. Other events in this room include a resident getting up in the middle of the night and asking to change rooms because they felt as though they were being strangled.

Room 6 – Disembodied footsteps, children giggling, and imprints on the quilt.

Room 8 – Described by the housekeeper as the most haunted room. When it's quiet, the housekeeper notices a child's handprint low down on the mirror, and an imprint of someone sitting down on one particular bed.

Room 8, described as the most active room by staff. (Author's collection)

Room 9 – Very cold 'whooshing' sensation – like a brisk breeze, with no explainable source.

Room 10 – Man checked out after first night, when someone sat on him in bed.

On conclusion of my hotel tour, I agreed with the staff to return with the rest of my paranormal team and carry out an investigation. That investigation took place just two weeks later.

The Investigation
The team met at the hotel just before closing time at 9 p.m. and, once the hotel was

The trigger objects being prepared as part of the investigation. (Author's collection)

all locked up, we set up the equipment. We had decided that, based on the testimonies from the staff, we would concentrate our investigation on the most active areas. This led to us focusing our attention on a small corridor outside the upper bar, the bar room itself, and Rooms 5 and 6. The other room that we included in our investigation was Room 8 on the second floor, as this was also known to be highly active and had been described by the housekeeper as the most haunted room. Our usual base reading tests were carried out and showed nothing particularly unusual – with the exception of quite a high EMF reading on the bed in Room 8. We checked around the room and were not able to find a source for this reading. Trigger objects were placed as follows:

☠ The corridor – Three balls (mixture in weight/size/colour) and a toy car

☠ Room 5 – A small plastic farm horse and some coins from the 1800s and 1900s

☠ Room 6 – Large wooden cross (because the site was once connected to the church)

☠ Room 8 – Teddy bear

I placed the items on paper and drew around them, inviting any resident children to play with them; we then sat down for a séance, led by Stuart. After a short prayer, conducted for the protection of participants, Stuart invited any spirit energies resident at the hotel to talk to us using the glass and board that we had set up. We all lightly placed one finger on the glass and, after a short while, it began to move around the board. Within minutes, a young boy introduced himself as Tim Frobisher. We started by playing a coin game with him to help him get used to moving the glass around the board – we placed coins on the board and invited him to knock them all off, which he did really well. He was a very strong energy and the glass moved quickly around the board. We then asked some questions about him and he told us that he had been nine years of age when he passed into spirit, in the year 1914, giving the cause of his passing as 'flu'. He also confirmed that he is very happy at the hotel (i.e. not grounded or in need of help) and that he resides there with his four siblings, giving their names as Harriet (four), Thomas (three), David (six) and Elvira (two).

He told us that although most of them had died young, David had actually lived until he was eighty-six, but upon passing had joined them at the hotel with the chosen age of six (presumably so they could all be together). We asked Tim about his parents and whether they had owned the hotel at the time of his passing. He gave his parents' names as Lenard and Mary, and said that they did not own the hotel – the family had just rented one room. He then said that his father had worked locally on the land as a rat catcher.

The glass then came to me, and Tim wrote, 'Moved toys.'

I smiled and said, 'Who has moved the toys?'

He replied, 'Me.'

I asked him which toys he had moved and he said, 'Big ball.' I looked at the large ball which was outside in the corridor. Whilst there was a possibility that it had been slightly moved, it had not moved completely off the marker that I had drawn, so I wasn't too excited – although I was pleased that he had seen where they all

were. I asked if his sisters liked the teddy I had left for them in Room 8 and he said, 'Yes.' He confirmed that Room 8 is where they spend most of their time. I also asked if he had seen the little horse, and struggled to remember which room I had left it in – at which point Tim reminded me it was Room 5!

Tim said that it is his handprint that people find on the mirror in Room 8. He told me they like to sit on the beds in there too. He also confirmed that the mysterious fire that took place in Room 5 was caused by a defective heater and they did not have anything to do with that.

In our final question to Tim, we sought clarification regarding the presence of any grown-ups in the hotel with him. He confirmed that in addition to the five children (himself and his siblings) there was one grown-up – a man. However, he said that he does not know or have anything to do with the spirit gentleman, so couldn't add any further details regarding his identity.

This photograph was taken during the séance. A large white orb was captured in the upper right of the picture.

This picture was taken when I invited our spirit friend Tim to appear with me. Could the large white glow on my top be Tim trying to show himself?

Tim was highly energetic when moving the glass around the board and, even though I am not spiritually gifted at all, I could really feel his happiness and playfulness coming through. He really seemed to enjoy his time talking with us. Of course, we were very grateful to him for all of the information he had given us, as we could now pass on this much-sought-after insight to the staff at the hotel, who have always felt affection towards the spirit children.

During the séance, I invited Tim to appear with me in a photograph. The glass moved to 'Yes', accepting my request, so I stood at the other side of the room and a team member took the picture on my camera. Upon inspection of that photograph, there appears to be quite a large white anomaly on the left side, on my clothing. There is also a very bright orb in one of the pictures that I took during the séance. Could these be images of Tim?

After safely closing down the séance, the team separated into smaller groups to carry out vigils in the most active areas, with the hope of capturing evidence or having a personal experience. Pam and I went to Room 8, where my EVP recorder had already been running throughout the investigation. We sat down in the dark, inviting the children to talk with us. The other team members remained in the upstairs bar. We did not personally experience anything during this time and, when our agreed vigil time period had ended, we concluded the investigation.

Séance Findings and Research

Tim described dying from flu, and records show that a worldwide pandemic of Spanish influenza broke out in 1918; between then and 1919 there were more deaths caused by flu than the war. However, this is not consistent with the year that he gave us. We often have difficulties obtaining accurate dates in séances, possibly because spirits have little recollection of dates – the spirit world is widely believed to be a place where time does not exist.

Having checked the dates of 1905 (birth) and 1914 (death), I was unable to find any record of Tim; this was disappointing as the séance had left no doubt in our minds about his identity – he had come through very strongly and concisely with his information. It is also a shame that, because they did not own the building, we are unable to validate the presence of the Frobisher family at the hotel.

EVP Evidence

We placed my EVP recorder in the upstairs bar while we were setting up, and a faint, but quite creepy, disembodied male voice was recorded saying, 'Where's the boy?'

We then set up our trigger objects and other equipment. My first stop was Room 8, where I left my EVP recorder. When reviewing the audio later, a child's voice was heard after thirty-one minutes, saying, 'Talking with Tim.' At this time in the investigation, we were still setting up equipment, and I was talking to the suspected spirit children as I went, explaining what our gadgets were for and inviting them to play with the toys. The photographs that we took during this process show a large white orb, which seemed to be following us around. At fifty-one minutes, in Room 8, another child's voice was recorded, very clearly, saying, 'We're watching you.' This sounded like a younger child and could be one of Tim's younger sisters. Another sound that was recorded in the room several times

A still of the EVP audio, showing the point (in the centre) where running footsteps were recorded. (Author's collection)

Top floor corridor of the hotel, where Room 8 is located. The large white orb seemed to be following us around on the night of the investigation and appeared in quite a few of the pictures.

throughout the evening was running footsteps. Tim's voice was not recorded much on the EVP recorder in Room 8 while the séance was ongoing. However, I would expect that, given that Tim was talking to us on the board for most of the séance.

During the vigil held in Room 8 with just Pam and I present, there were no unusual sounds recorded. However, right at the end of the audio, you hear me say, 'OK, we're switching off now … Bye Tim. Bye anyone else that's in here,' and a child's voice says, 'Bye bye Gem.' This brought tears to my eyes when I played it back afterwards because I would have loved to have heard it at the time. I am not psychic but I did feel a warm connection with the little boy Tim; he really was lovely. When we closed down the investigation, I made it clear to him that he would have to stay in the hotel because that is where he belongs – but I did promise to go back and visit him again, and I definitely will.

Conclusion

The investigation was most enjoyable, and it was very comforting for both our investigation team and the staff at the hotel to learn that the resident spirits were not in any distress. It is also nice for the staff to

Fellow team members from SPI (Spalding Paranormal Investigations). Standing: Josh Stretton and Chris Joyce. Seated: Stuart Moulder and Pam Stretton.

that there is high potential for capturing further evidence in the future.

The collective findings of the investigation validate the testimonies that we were given prior to our investigation, which is a good result – although it was disappointing that none of the toys were moved off the markers I had set, despite what Tim had said about having moved them. I am further intrigued by the orb phenomenon, especially the large orb that appeared on my clothing when I asked Tim to appear in a photograph with me. However, I am disappointed that I was not able to see a full body apparition – perhaps I set my expectations too high!

In summary, is the Chequers Hotel haunted? Absolutely YES! But I prefer to use the term 'active' because it is filled with warm, happy and playful energy.

finally know the identities of the spirit children who live alongside them.

Based on the evidence that we found, it is not possible to validate or research Tim's story further. That said, I was pleased with the quality of the evidence as a whole. Whilst the overall levels of EMF around the hotel were low to non-existent, we had extremely high EMF levels on the bed in Room 8 whilst taking our base readings and during the investigation – and then found out during the séance that the children often sit on the bed in this room. We also had anomalies appearing in our photographs, the sound of a gentleman's voice, good clear voices of children, and the sound of their footsteps in Room 8 captured on the EVP recorders. This is fantastic evidence. Given that we were only investigating the hotel for one evening and activity is frequently reported there, I feel

Holbeach Sports & Social Club

Holbeach Sports & Social Club was established in 1982; the site consists of a large football ground, a lounge/bar and a large function hall. I was approached by the owners, Mr and Mrs Spencer, who have been connected with the site for the last ten years and have experienced a lot of unusual events during that time. For many years Mrs Spencer has wondered if the activity is paranormal, having been unable to find other explanations, and the couple have even affectionately named their suspected ghost 'Matey'. In addition to sharing their story and experiences with me, they hoped that I would be able to shed some light on the events – particularly as Mr Spencer is a non-believer in anything paranormal.

I met them at the club and we began by looking at when it all started. The first strange thing that happened was that, on

Holbeach Sports & Social Club. (Author's collection)

a few occasions when opening up in the morning, light bulbs would 'shoot' out of their fittings and fly across the room. The lights would also frequently flicker. Another thing noticed by cleaners was that, upon unlocking the building, they would sometimes find the taps running and the heaters on; these things are meticulously checked by Mr and Mrs Spencer when they lock up each night and staff have therefore struggled to find an explanation. One day an event occurred while all the staff were present – some sink taps suddenly started to run 'on their own'; the owner said to the cleaners and other staff, 'Perhaps you believe me now when I say we don't leave them on!'

Mrs Spencer also recalled an incident when 'something' pulled on her trousers and even touched her bottom. At the time she thought it was her husband, but when she turned round she was shocked to realise that there was no one there, which left her feeling quite unsettled. Another female member of staff was pushed by an unknown force while on the premises. In addition, a male apparition has been spotted on site and in the building by two female members of staff and by a previous investigator.

Mrs Spencer confided her suspicion that there could be a male spirit (or possibly more than one) present in the building, who likes playing jokes and interacting with them. Other forms of interaction she has experienced include the ice machine mysteriously turning off or objects going missing; when these incidents occur, she says, 'OK, you've had your fun now.' Upon saying these words, the ice machine will mysteriously switch itself back on and

The function hall, where missing objects appear in the middle of the stage. High EMF readings were recorded at a particular table and several orb-like anomalies were captured in photographs. (Author's collection)

the missing objects will reappear somewhere completely unexpected. The staff informed me that it was not just their own belongings that would go missing – a lady once visited the football club to run a fitness session, using an iPod to play the music. Following the session, the instructor realised that her iPod was missing and staff turned the club upside down to find it. After a fruitless search, Mrs Spencer joked that 'Matey' probably had it and she asked out loud for him to give it back. The following morning, she was amazed to discover that it had reappeared in the middle of the stage. Other activity reported here includes glasses 'shooting' from shelves and smashing on the floor, gas being switched off in the cellar and doors slamming shut.

In an attempt to get to the bottom of the paranormal activity at the social club,

the owners invited a medium to attend one evening, in the presence of many friends and members of the local community, to try to connect with any spirits in the building. On the night in question, the medium was carrying a microphone as he paced the building, inviting the spirit energies to come forward. The onlookers reported that in addition to the medium's voice, they could hear the faint sound of other voices coming through the speakers, although the words were not decipherable. Unfortunately, the spirit(s) that walk the building were reluctant to communicate with the medium, which left everyone quite disappointed as they were keen to learn more about the activity and its perpetrator(s).

The medium resorted to provocation techniques in order to encourage communication and, as he sat around a table with the owners, he said out loud, 'I think your football team is crap.' Apparently, upon saying these words the table tipped up, the lights started to vigorously flicker, and it became clear to everyone that the spirit was there and had become annoyed. Sadly, when the evening ended, no one was any the wiser about the identity of the spirit(s) in the building or the motives behind the activity. The medium offered to return for a night-time vigil on a separate occasion, but wanted payment to do so and the owners didn't really want to take that route.

I do not personally agree with spirit provocation as I believe they should be respected in the same way as people. Furthermore, if they do not want to come through and talk then they won't. I spoke at length with the staff about this issue, as my investigation techniques are somewhat different. I went on to explain that aside from the séances, the team investigate by using technology to try to capture hard evidence of the activity taking place. I always stress that whilst I am a strong believer in the paranormal, my main objective in investigating is to find evidence of paranormal activity that could convince a sceptic and, where possible, gain insight on the cause of the activity. Given that my team does not charge people to do this, Mr and Mrs Spencer were very keen for us to return at a later date.

It is noteworthy that during my initial visit to the football club, I had some strange experiences of my own; I had taken some of my investigation gadgets along with me, as I usually do, and, whilst sitting around a table discussing the strange phenomena taking place, the lights on the walls around us started to dim and flicker. Around this time, my EMF detector also started to record high levels of random electromag-

netic energy, which can be attributable to manifestation.

Furthermore, when I took out my camera to take some photographs, it immediately started to malfunction in a way that it never has previously. The lens and shutter began opening then closing in a continuous movement and, once open, the camera would not focus – then an error message would pop up telling me to switch it off then on again. I tried cleaning the lens/shutter area and taking out the battery, but none of these actions were successful in getting it to function normally. Finally, I abandoned the idea of taking photographs and decided to explore other areas of the building. Having explained to the staff and any resident spirits how my equipment works, I began exploring the function hall. Suddenly, the KII began to register very high readings of EMF – at one particular table and on the chairs that surrounded it. There was no wiring or source of electricity in close proximity; however, the function hall did have a lot of lights and wiring by the dance floor, which could have contributed to the high readings. I knew that it was going to be difficult to distinguish spirit interaction from general spikes of electromagnetic energy. That said, the KII did seem to light up when we were talking about 'Matey', and it did light up and go back to green several times on request.

The Investigation

In order to investigate the football club thoroughly, I wanted to look at each individual occurrence in case some events could be disregarded; when you are in the mindset that you live or work in a haunted building, it is easy to put every unusual occurrence down to 'the ghost' when there might be other explanations. I always stress the importance of investigating objectively, because it is only when you remain objective that you can definitely confirm the extent of paranormal activity and establish whether a building is truly haunted or not.

On the night of the investigation, several guests were invited who wanted to observe or take part in the séance. We set up the equipment at 8.30 p.m. and carried out our usual baseline readings – as suspected, they showed high levels of EMF in the function hall. We were mindful that the wiring and lights in that particular room would have been a contributory factor in this; however, there were also very strong intermittent readings in the bar area at the other side of the building, and there was no obvious source for those. As before, the machine seemed to light up to orange and flicker vigorously in this area – but only when we were talking about the paranormal activity. We also noticed the lights on the wall flickering when we were talking about the possibility of resident spirits.

A séance was set up in the function room and Stuart recited a short prayer for the protection of all participants. The guests were sitting around the table, many participating, as we invited any resident spirit energies to come forward and speak with us. We assured them that we meant them no harm and only wanted to find out more about them. An EMF detector and voice recorder were also operational at the table, and the EMF detector would seemingly light up every time Mrs Spencer joked about the ghost pinching her bottom!

The Séance

The first energy that came to talk to us on the board confirmed itself to be a female and gave her name. I have opted not to publish that particular detail as her year of passing was relatively recent (1990), but she confirmed herself to be a happy spirit and not in need of help. Mrs Spencer was stunned to learn that it was in fact this spirit who was responsible for pinching her bottom and also for some of the other pranks encountered at the club. That said, the spirit lady did mention that she had a gentleman with her who visited the club and was a bit of a prankster.

Following our conversation with the spirit lady, we were joined by the energy of a little boy. He told us that his name was David Adams but he preferred to be called Davey. He said that he had passed into spirit in 1796, at the age of seven, as a result of scurvy (brought about by poor diet). When questioned, he confirmed that his home used to be on the site of the football club. He described himself as a 'rascal' and said that he likes to move things about and play jokes on people; he also claimed that he

The séance in the function hall. Four coins were positioned in a line by the spirit boy, who likes to be known as Davey. (Author's collection)

has pinched someone's bottom and, when asked to take the glass to the person that he pinched, he took the glass to Mrs Spencer. We invited Davey to play the coin game and he consented, so we placed four coins around the board and asked him to knock them all off. He enjoyed that experience and wanted to do it again; the second time, he pushed all of the coins into the middle of the board to form a line.

After a short intermission, the séance was moved to the pub area, where we once again connected with David and the female resident spirit; some personal connections were also made among participants. After safe closure of the séance, we closed the investigation and went away to review the findings.

The mysterious white glow picked up on the CCTV image. During the investigation, it was confirmed to have been caused by a cracked camera lens rather than one of the resident spirits. (Author's collection)

Debunking Exercise

The staff at the club had been concerned about a strange white anomaly that had appeared on their CCTV camera and, given the high levels of activity that they experience, wondered if it had a paranormal explanation. I had taken a photograph of it on my initial visit to the club because I wanted to examine it more closely and, upon establishing with the owners that the image never moves and always appears in the same place, I suspected that it would probably have a scientific and logical explanation. While the séance was ongoing, a team member looked at this in more detail, in order to establish whether a problem with the camera or an external lighting source was causing the eerie white blob. Upon close examination of the CCTV camera, the lens was found to be cracked.

Following this exercise, some coins were set up in the now empty bar on the other side of the building, with a voice recorder left alongside. Spirit energies were invited to knock down or move the coins and leave us messages. We chose coins because the staff at the club had previously informed us of several strange events involving coins being moved, balanced or thrown.

Evidence and Conclusion

It would be fantastic if we could prove that David did exist in the time period he gave us. However, given that he claimed to be from the late 1700s, it would be very difficult to validate his story through records available today. There were nine energies in total that visited the séance (although some were connected to people rather than the club); good validation was given by some of the spirits, when they correctly answered very specific questions and the answers were only known to the enquirer.

Upon reviewing the audio from the investigation, I heard a few voices – some speaking at unusual times or over our own voices – where the sound seemed to be close to the microphone but on a different sound frequency. However, I was unable to

Lounge/bar area, where much of the paranormal activity occurs. (Author's collection)

pin-point any decipherable electronic voice phenomena on this occasion, which was disappointing. It was difficult to find the right location within the building for good EVP, as the function hall was acoustically very echoey and absolute silence was not achievable anywhere due to the number of people present for the séance. There was also noise contamination in the pub area, where humming from nearby appliances came through very strongly on the audio. It could be possible to carry out further EVP work in the social club; however, it would have to be under very carefully controlled conditions.

The function hall is typically colder than in the pub; however, during the investigation temperature drops were noted in the pub, with a few people (myself included) reporting a cold feeling around their legs.

Many of the photographs taken throughout the investigation show large white orbs and, whilst the jury is out as to whether they will ever be considered evidence of the paranormal, it is noteworthy that during the séance, when we became aware that there were nine spirit energies in the room, a photograph was taken and nine white orbs were visible in that picture.

Regrettably, the coins that were left on a table for the spirits to move were not interfered with at all. However, despite the lack of physical evidence of paranormal activity, the investigation was successful in the sense that Mr and Mrs Spencer gained the information that they had wanted for so long. Now, instead of saying 'Matey', they will be able to address the spirits by their true names – and the fact that the two strongest presences are actually a lady and a seven-year-old boy came as a big surprise to them. Of course, there is also a gentleman spirit that pops in from time to time, which explains the male apparition that has been seen on the premises. In summary, I would have to say that I do strongly believe the club is haunted – it's hard to ignore testimonies from so many different people. I would love an opportunity in the future to capture further evidence of the spirit activity.

The Mansion House, High Street, Holbeach

The Mansion House is thought to have been built in 1681 and was once home to the 1933 Nobel Peace Prize winner Sir Norman Angell. Having been a family home for centuries, the listed building was

The Mansion House Hotel, Holbeach. (Courtesy of Googlemaps ©2011 Google-Map Data © 2011 Tele Atlas)

extensively and lovingly renovated into an elegant hotel five years ago. Despite the scale of the alterations, it still retains original timbers, seventeenth-century features and a historic atmosphere.

Some of the strange sightings reported at the Mansion House Hotel have led the local community, staff and some of the guests to believe that previous occupants of the building may still be residing there. The most common sighting is that of a woman, aged approximately thirty-five, looking out of the top right-hand window. The hotel holds regular psychic evenings with medium Julia Farmer; she told me that on her very first evening working in the hotel, with no prior knowledge of the previously reported sightings, she was immediately drawn to look up at the upper right-hand window as she pulled up in her car – upon doing so she could see a presence in the room. She could not see detail, but she returned on another day to investigate further. On that visit, she immediately connected with a lady and felt fear associated with her – as though she was frightened of her husband. She could also smell cigar smoke in the corridor outside the room, and this smell has sometimes been noted by other people.

One gentleman who has reported seeing the ghostly lady in the window also had a strange experience at the Mansion House while undertaking a painting job with a friend many years ago. They were the only two people in the building other than the owner. Thirsty and in need of a tea break, they left their tins of paint at the top of the stairs, with the lids still on them, and went downstairs. Upon returning a short while later, however, the lids had all been removed from the tins, the brushes were inside the paint pots and the pots themselves had been moved to the bottom of the stairs. Very con-

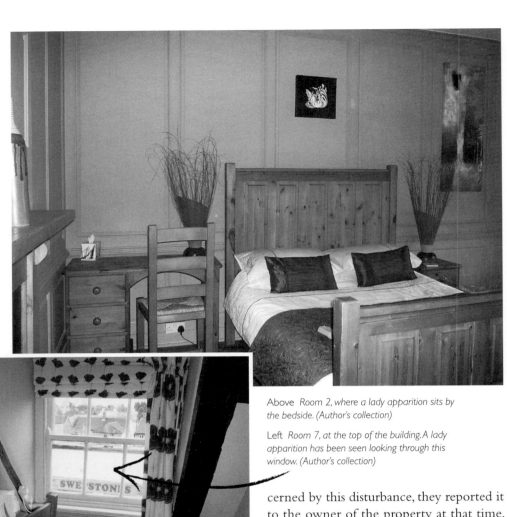

Above *Room 2, where a lady apparition sits by the bedside. (Author's collection)*

Left *Room 7, at the top of the building. A lady apparition has been seen looking through this window. (Author's collection)*

cerned by this disturbance, they reported it to the owner of the property at that time, whose cheery response was, 'Oh! So you've met our friend then?' Apparently the family residing there were very familiar with the resident ghost and had come to accept the many pranks that were played on them.

A solicitor once stayed in Room 3 of the hotel. In the middle of the night he heard the door handle turn; then the door itself opened. Looking up, he was absolutely terrified to see a woman standing over him. Several guests have reported this experience and guests staying in Room 2 and Room 5 have reported similar incidents. Sometimes they report seeing a woman sitting at their bedside.

Previous owners of the property have also commented that they used to wake up in the middle of the night to find their shower running; this was extremely bizarre as it had a heavy Victorian-style lever that they had to pull round to turn on and off, so there was no way it could turn on by accident. They would also hear their toilet flush in the middle of the night when no one was using it.

Whilst walking round the hotel with Julia and the owner Richard, I had my EMF detector, voice recorder and camera. A significant white orb was captured on my camera by the bed in Room 2. The EMF detector reacted to some of the requests to communicate and, interestingly, it was also detecting the presence of spirits in places where Julia sensed a spirit was standing. Furthermore, when I played back the audio recording from my visit, I could hear voices belonging to a male and a female – the voices were clearly on a different frequency to ours. The two decipherable EVP that were recorded came from Room 3 and were as follows:

Julia: 'Are you in here now?'
Male voice: 'YES'
Random male voice: 'You're good for nowt.'

The lady's voice was faintly audible at times throughout the recording, but unfortunately I was not able to pick out any clear EVP because much of the time it was 'underneath' our own conversation. And, in view of the fact that the purpose of my visit was to walk around the building and talk about the resident spirits, much of the recording is contaminated by footsteps and talking. However, I will definitely be returning to the Mansion House to carry out further EVP work.

The String of Horses Inn, Boston Road, Holbeach

The String of Horses is a seventeenth-century coaching inn. It was originally a one-storey building, where travellers would stop off for ale, and perhaps a bowl of soup, before continuing their journey. Approximately 170 years ago, an upper floor was added to the building, and it was used as a function hall and bar for some years before recently being converted into hotel accommodation. Adjacent to this, on the upper floor, is a flat where pub owners have resided over the years.

During my visit to the String of Horses, the current owner, Richard Rickerby, described always feeling uncomfortable when locking up the function hall – an eerie sensation of being watched. He said that he would switch off all the lights, lock the doors and hurry back downstairs as quickly as possible, away from the strange atmosphere. His uncomfortable feeling was further fuelled by the fact that, on many occasions, he would return upstairs to find the lights all switched on again. Also, locking up the pub itself could make him feel

The String of Horses. (Courtesy of Google Maps ©2011 Google)

The corridor outside the accommodation area on the upper floor, formerly a function room. I asked any resident spirits to appear in the pictures and, after a few clicks of the camera, bright white orbs started to appear. (Author's collection)

up to watch TV. Every time this happened, she would find the living space empty and the children sound asleep in bed.

I spent some time on the upper floor of the String of Horses during my visit, and noticed immediately that there were a lot of random spikes of electromagnetic energy. There was no source for these at all, given that much of the power was disconnected at the time. Furthermore, the EMF detector seemed to be reacting to questions that we were asking, as well as spiking up to orange upon our requests to light up. Interestingly, the responsive spikes on the EMF meter seemed to follow us around the corridor, into what are now hotel rooms, and the machine lit up next to me when I sat down on the bed. The most active area for consistent EMF readings, however, was in the exact location where the upstairs bar used to be. Richard strongly believes that there are a few happy spirits resident in the pub who either worked there or spent many years drinking there; he has speculated that they love it so much they don't want to leave! He reiterated that nothing scary happens in the building, which leads him to conclude that the energies present are friendly, and it was merely the feeling of being watched over the years that made him feel uncomfortable. During the interview, I invited any spirits present to speak to us on the digital voice recorder, just in case any of them were in need of help.

When my visit ended, I agreed to check the audio recording and let Richard know if anything unusual had been captured. When I listened to it, I was concerned to hear that two EVP had been picked up. A man, who seemed to be in distress, could be distinctly heard saying 'Get me out of here' and 'Hurt me'. Hearing this on the recording made me consider the possibility that the spirit gentleman was trapped and unable to move on.

uncomfortable. Sometimes, upon locking the door and walking away, two brooms that had been leaning up against a wall would fall down. The brooms were always positioned very securely and were nowhere near him.

An unusual occurrence that has been noticed by several people is the sound of disembodied footsteps emanating from the flat on the upper floor of the pub. The lady who used to live there stated that she would often hear heavy footsteps walking along the hallway. Often, she would get out of bed at night and check the living room, thinking that one of her children had got

The Granary, Market Street, Long Sutton. (Author's collection)

He could have been tampering with the lights and brooms to make his presence felt, in the hope of getting help to move on. I therefore sent Richard the EVP that I had found and he immediately contacted medium Julia Farmer. Julia went to the String of Horses a few days later in order to 'clear' the premises, giving the troubled spirit the help that he needed to pass over peacefully.

The Granary Hotel, Bar & Restaurant, Market Street, Long Sutton

Previously a pub called the Corn Exchange, this building was beautifully renovated into a contemporary bar, restaurant and hotel. It is first recorded in the 1881 census, although the exact date of construction is unclear. Although the building has always been a public house, over the years part of it has been used for various commercial outlets and has seen numerous changes to the layout. However, besides a change of colour, it has retained much of its original fabric and character on the outside – and also seems to have retained a mysterious character on the inside!

The ghostly activity began three years ago when, following the closure of the Corn Exchange, the building remained unoccupied for some time before being taken over, renovated and reopened as the Granary. During the renovation, workers took down part of the ceiling and were stunned to discover a large area of roof space which had remained undisturbed for many years. The roof space became part of the restaurant. Staff members experience an uncomfortable feeling whilst laying out cutlery in this area. One lady in particular said that she has felt as though someone is standing over her, watching her. Some of the staff will not venture into the upper restaurant on their own.

Whilst the paranormal activity in the Granary does not affect the hotel, it is by no means restricted to the upper restaurant.

The upper restaurant, where staff frequently feel an oppressive presence. (Author's collection)

Several staff members have reported hearing someone calling out their name from the cellar; when they ask who it is, it transpires that no one called them at all. On my visit, I spoke at length with the chef who, despite having only worked in his role for four weeks, has had several unexplainable experiences. The first unusual thing he noticed was that often on a Sunday, when he would arrive for work at 6 a.m. and enter through the back door of the pub, he would see a shadow go out of the front door. Also, he would hear sounds coming from the cellar, even though he knew that no one could be there because he is completely on his own in the building at that time. Usually when he hears the sounds it is very early in the morning; other staff members have said it can also be late at night,

when the building is very quiet. Another thing the chef has noticed is that he frequently arrives at work to find the gas hob turned on and, while he is working alone in the building, he feels a presence.

I was keen to experience the activity myself and check out the possible sources of 'movement' in the cellar, so I visited the Granary late one evening with another member of my team, equipped with an EVP recorder, camera and EMF detector.

Our first vigil took place in the cellar and, despite all of the appliances down there, the EMF meter did not seem to react to anything at all. I did a sweep round all the units, appliances, ceiling and floor to check the sensitivity levels on the meter and, aside from a couple of the major appliances, nothing really set it off. Having set up our equipment, we explained to any spirits present what our gadgets were for and invited them to talk to us or light up our EMF meter. After a short while, it lit up slightly when I was standing in the middle of the room. Responding to this, I said 'hello' and invited the spirit to use my energy to take the lights up to orange – at that very moment, the orange light came on, and remained on for several seconds. As I moved the detector around to try to establish the size of the spirit, I noted that the lights were only illuminated from my waist down – when I took the detector above this level, the lights went out. With three of the lights illuminated, I invited the spirit to take them all the way to red. At this moment the orange light began to flicker, then completely illuminated again. I felt that the spirit was struggling to do this. I then asked them to step back from the machine. At this moment, the light display reverted back to its standard reading of one green light. When I invited the spirit to come forward again and light it up, the machine lit up to orange – as before, only from my waist down to the floor.

This happened twice during our cellar vigil and I was very intrigued by the fact that the lights seemed to be going on and off on command. It raised the possibility of an intelligent spirit being present – and, given the height and area of the EMF readings, I suspected that this was the spirit of a child.

I took some photographs in the cellar and two large orbs were captured in the area where the EMF readings had been picked up. Upon reviewing the EVP recordings, I picked up something even more interesting; at one stage, you can hear me say, 'We're not here to scare you, we would just love to know who you are.' In response, a child's voice says, 'Yes Miss.'

This EVP was quite loud and very clear – a fantastic result, strongly supporting the possibility of a child spirit being present.

The vigil in the restaurant resulted in very significant illuminations of the EMF detector, which we had placed on one of the tables. Given that the staff had reported feeling as though they were 'being watched', I checked for electromagnetic energy emanating from possible nearby sources. The upper restaurant, where the oppressive feelings are reported, is very small and, if energy levels were particularly high as a result of wiring, lighting or other appliances, then anyone spending a significant amount of time in that area could experience those symptoms. I did not, however, find any obvious source to account for the readings.

The EMF detector lit up all the way to red several times whilst on the table, seeming to happen when we were inviting the spirits to talk to us, as well as on cue when we were asking questions. It is noteworthy that my team member and I felt very comfortable sitting in the upper restaurant, and did not experience any negative or oppressive feeling. The photographs and EMF readings, though, suggest we may not have been on our own!

I would definitely like to revisit the Granary to carry out further investigation work, as we had some very good interaction in the short time we spent there. Maybe one day we will be able to shed more light on who roams the building after closing time.

The Old Black Lion, Gedney

I made contact with the owners of this 1750s public house and restaurant following reports that various people had seen the

The Old Black Lion. (Author's collection)

apparition of a little boy, in period clothing, playing by the fireplace. Upon contacting the owners, they confirmed the reports to be true and told me about a few of their own encounters in the pub. Apparently, objects would often go missing and mysteriously reappear in a different place, and the radio would switch itself on and off. The chef also frequently felt a 'presence' in the kitchen – although the staff emphasised that the feeling was never unpleasant and none of the strange events ever made them feel uncomfortable.

Following my discussions with the staff, the paranormal team that I was working with at the time returned to carry out a full investigation. We were keen to find out the identity of the mysterious spirit boy, establish whether any other spirits were present in the building, find out who was responsible for moving the objects, and hopefully capture some evidence.

When we arrived on the day of the investigation, we were informed by the owners that there had been another incident – earlier that day, in fact – involving an object going missing. The landlady had left her magazine on the bar, only to find that it had gone when she returned a few moments later. A gentleman sitting in the pub at the time informed her that he had seen a little boy in period clothing take it. The incident had occurred close to the fireplace, and this development left me highly intrigued and very excited about the upcoming investigation.

The owners of the pub had invited some of the local community to join us for the investigation, as many of them had seen or heard about the little boy; there had been folklore for many years about a boy who had fallen down the steps in the cellar to his death. We were happy for the locals to join us, although we are always mindful that

the presence of too many people can cause noise contamination during the scientific parts of the investigation – particularly the EVP work, as the digital recorders that we use are very sensitive and some spirit voices are quiet when they come through on the recording. I need to know when I review the tapes that I am hearing a spirit voice and not that of someone else in the building. The EVP work really has to be done under carefully controlled conditions with no other people around.

To begin the investigation I went down to the cellar, assisted by a local resident, and placed trigger objects on the floor,

Left *Entrance to the cellar, where folklore tells of a little boy who fell to his death many years ago. (Author's collection)*

Below *The Old Black Lion. The fireplace where the little boy in period dress was seen playing on numerous occasions by several customers. (Author's collection)*

inviting any children that might be present to play with them. I set up a camera to record any movement. I then began my EVP work by introducing myself and inviting any spirits to come forward and talk to me. I also asked specific questions, in the hope of receiving answers from an 'intelligent' spirit presence. The cellar door was closed and it was pitch black; we maintained these controlled conditions throughout the investigation.

While this was going on, there were two séances simultaneously taking place in different rooms of the pub – I should add, nowhere near the cellar – and amongst the many spirit visitors who came through to speak to us was a little boy who attended both séances at different stages during the evening. He said that his name was Alan and that he had passed into spirit at the age of six, following an accident when he had fallen down the cellar steps. He confirmed that he liked to move objects about and, when questioned, he admitted that he had taken the magazine and said he would give it back. Most importantly of all, he said that he was a happy spirit who enjoyed visiting the pub.

It was fantastic to receive communication from the little boy at the séances. In addition, when we reviewed the EVP audio afterwards, there were a few very clear electronic voice phenomena. In one of them, you can hear me say, 'I'm just going to take some photographs of your lovely building, so leave me a message while I'm gone and when I get back I'll pick it up.' A child's voice is then heard saying, 'See you Gem!' This brought tears to my eyes when I heard it back. He sounded like such a chirpy little boy and it's a shame I could not hear him at the time!

While I was taking photographs, at approximately 1 a.m., a further EVP was recorded. It was the sound of an elderly lady saying, 'Morning!' I was surprised at how loud and clear this one was. There was one more, quite loud, sound recorded in the cellar, which sounds like a child laughing.

The investigation that we carried out at the Old Black Lion was extremely fruitful. Moreover, a few days later the owners confirmed to me that the magazine taken on the day of the investigation had mysteriously reappeared. The local community really enjoyed the evening and, now that people know the identity of the playful spirit boy, everyone can refer to him by name.

The Farm, Broadgate, Weston Hills

Several years ago, when a farmer named Henry resided alone at the farm, a strange incident occurred one night that he could not explain and could never forget. It marked the beginning of several mysterious occurrences and the revelation of a special connection.

This still from the EVP recording shows heightened sound waves, depicting the moment when the very audible child's laughter was captured.

On the night in question, Henry was awakened by the presence of a woman standing at the foot of his bed. She stood motionless, just looking at him; he gazed up at her and immediately noticed that not only had the room become very noticeably colder, but the woman was dressed in clothing from a much earlier time. He had never had any special interest in ghosts or the paranormal, but he knew straightaway that the lady he was looking at was not of this world. Whilst he was trying to make sense of this visual spectacle, the lady vanished – in the blink of an eye.

In the years that followed, Henry met his partner, Louise, and she moved into the house. There had been no further sightings and Henry never talked about the ghostly lady – until one day, when Louise saw something extraordinary. It was a warm, August afternoon and she was playing tennis in the court within the grounds of the farm. The court is surrounded by a high hedge, which blocks the view to the surrounding fields, but there is a small gap in the hedge which is closed by a white picket fence. On this particular day, Henry was just about to serve the ball to Louise when she became distracted by a lady behind him, standing in the gap of the hedge and looking straight at them. The lady did not speak and Louise could tell that she was from a different era. She described the lady apparition as being in her thirties with mousy brown hair, wearing a cream-coloured fitted top and a floor-length skirt which had a swirly pattern on it. Louise did not feel threatened by the lady, but her gaze had made her feel quite shaken. When Henry served the ball to her she missed it – still staring at the lady behind him. He served the ball again and she distractedly hit it into the net. At this time, Henry noticed that the temperature of the air around him had considerably dropped, to the extent that it was freezing cold and no longer felt like a summer's day. He said to Louise, 'You've just seen something haven't you?' Louise told him about the lady. By this time the lady apparition had completely vanished but, upon comparing Louise's sighting with his own, Henry was able to say with much certainty that they had both seen the same lady – although neither of them had recognised her and they had no idea who she was.

Following this incident, they saw the lady on the stairs in the house, and reflected in a mirror on their stairs. On those occasions, it happened so quickly that by the time they registered her presence she had vanished again. Furthermore, there have been disembodied footsteps and a loud crashing sound around the home, and objects have been moved. When Henry was decorating one of the rooms, he was keeping the door tightly shut overnight because of the smell of the paint – but on more than one occasion he would get up in the morning and notice that the door had been opened.

Louise's eldest son also had a strange experience in the house. The headphones to his iPod went missing and he was unable to find them after spending several days searching. Then, one morning when no one else was in the house, he was in the bathroom cleaning his teeth when he heard something drop on the floor behind him. When he looked down he was stunned to see his headphones at his feet.

The family never felt uncomfortable in the house because they sensed that the ghost was not a negative presence, despite not knowing her identity; however, a recent revelation has shed a lot of light on the strange occurrences that they have experienced over the years. A spiritualist gentleman whom Louise is connected to through her work approached her and said, 'You have a lady visiting your house don't you?'

Louise said, 'Erm … yes, we think we do.'

The gentleman said, 'It's a great-great-aunt of Henry.' He even gave the name Emily – and her surname. He described her appearance and it was exactly as Louise recalled from her sighting in the tennis court; he added that Emily was just watching over them. Quite intrigued by the idea of gaining insight into the unusual events at their home, Louise gave Henry this information. He was quite adamant that there was no one with the name Emily on his side of the family, but he asked his sisters to check nonetheless. A few days later, he was stunned to be contacted by his sister with the information that there had been a great-great-aunt called Emily. Emily had died in approximately 1935 and records showed that the surname given by the spiritualist was correct. The spiritualist had also said that there was a picture of Emily somewhere in the family and, when Henry tracked down the picture, he was immediately able to confirm that it was the lady that had been visiting their home.

The family now feel immensely comforted to know that their Emily is watching over them; although, since discovering the identity of their lady ghost, there have not been any further sightings of her.

The Crown Inn, Gosberton Road, Surfleet

This former coaching inn, built in approximately 1796, apparently showed no obvious signs of paranormal activity until the present owner, Zara Foster, moved in fifteen years ago. Upon taking ownership of what was then a modern pub, she

was keen to restore the building in a way that would be reminiscent of its history. It is since this restoration work that the unusual spirit encounters have occurred.

Current testimonies indicate that there are at least three spirit presences in the Crown Inn: two children have been seen on numerous occasions and an adult presence has been sensed on the upstairs landing. The adult is thought to be male – a young family member woke in the night and reported that a ghost gentleman had been stroking his head and saying 'Sssh!'. On another occasion a large impression was made on one of the upstairs beds, as though someone was lying on it. Presences are certainly felt both upstairs and downstairs, although never have they felt oppressive, threatening or negative.

Zara recalled one visual spectacle that occurred downstairs while she was changing a barrel in the cellar. Prior to entering the cellar she had been sweeping, and had left the broom propped up against the bar. Later, she looked up and saw that the broom had not only moved down to the cellar but was standing bolt upright! She ran to fetch another member of staff, who also witnessed this bizarre event.

During my visit to the pub I was intrigued by the presence of the children, and especially the story surrounding sightings of a little girl. In the early years of Zara's occupation of the Crown Inn, she had been talking with a local customer, explaining her plans for transforming a small raised area in the pub (a former bottling area) that used to lead down to the cellar. As she spoke to the gentleman, he became transfixed on the feature fireplace and started crying. Overcome with emotion, he exclaimed that he could see a little girl standing there, next to the decorative fireplace. Her hair was blonde and styled in ringlets, she wore a black dress with a white pinafore, and she was making flower posies. He estimated that her age was about nine. The little girl was also seen on a later date by a woman at a karaoke evening. The woman kept staring in that direction and, when questioned by Zara, she described the same girl. The spirit has since been seen by several other people.

That area of the pub once housed a piano, which Zara's daughter used to play. The area was always described as 'too cold', being unusually colder than the rest of the building. On one occasion, a young boy visited the pub and played on the piano. Later that day, after he had gone, both Zara and a male lodger sitting in the bar area heard singing and piano music. Baffled, they followed the mysterious music and were led to the area where the piano was situated. To their astonishment, the piano was playing all by itself. The keys were not moving but the sound was definitely emanating from the piano. As they listened intently, they recognised it to be the same tune that the little boy had been playing earlier. At this moment their attention was drawn to the right of the piano, where they could see the middle part of a little girl swaying contentedly in time with the music.

The little girl has now been seen on at least five separate occasions by different individuals. It is believed that she passed away in 1806 when she was run over by a stagecoach on the main road. It is thought that the little boy spirit (who is sometimes seen around the cellar) is her brother. Zara recalled that she was once in the cellar and saw the lower legs and feet of what she believed to be her grandson standing at the top of the steps – the rest of the body was obscured by the low ceiling. Concerned for his safety, she shouted, 'Stay where you are!' and ran to rescue him – but upon going upstairs there was no trace of her grandson, and it transpired that he had been in another room for some time with another family member!

The spirits at the Crown Inn make their presence known by moving objects, playing with lights and appearing as bright white orbs in photographs – but the staff and Zara's family are very happy to share their living space with them, and there has never been any indication that the entities are unhappy.

The piano is now located in the restaurant. As I took photographs in this area, I invited the spirits to appear in them. Several orb-like anomalies were captured.

Afterword

For as long as I can remember, I have had a passion for listening to people's ghostly testimonies, researching different theories relating to manifestations, and eventually investigating haunted locations first-hand on a quest to capture evidence of paranormal activity and the afterlife. I have now investigated many haunted locations, locally and further afield, and there are still so many that I have yet to explore. Like other investigators all over the world, I hope that I will one day be able to capture physical evidence, irrefutable to the most hardened of sceptics, of the existence of ghosts.

I have met many wonderful people throughout the course of writing this book and the most common questions I have been asked are, 'Have you ever had a ghostly experience?' and 'Don't you get scared?' Well, I have to be honest and in both cases say, 'Absolutely yes!' They say spirits can't harm you, but unpredictable events such as the hurling of a tonic bottle over a counter and people being physically pushed seem to contradict that theory and, whilst nothing of that nature has happened to me so far, you have to expect the unexpected when out on investigations. It can be a little unnerving sitting in dark cellars inviting spirits to come and interact with me, or walking around creaky, dark, unfamiliar places during the night using my various gadgets to attract the attention of ghosts. However, my passion for capturing evidence far exceeds the fear factor and I have to say that if I came face-to-face with a ghost now I would be scrambling for my investigation gadgets rather than the nearest exit! As I continue on my journey for answers and evidence, I hope people will enjoy reading the ghostly experiences and stories that are contained within the pages of this book. And I would like to leave you with this chilling thought: statistically, more non-believers and sceptics will have a ghostly experience in their lifetime than those who believe; but whether you are a believer or non-believer, how would you react if any of the spooky events from this book happened to you?

Gemma King, 2012

Bibliography

Arnold, N., *Long Sutton in Times Past* (Countryside Publications Ltd, 1984)

Bevis, Trevor, *Snippets from Old Spalding Town* (self-published, 1994)

Carroll, Ray; Martin, Ernie; Tingey, Ray; Tingle, Joyce; Waltham, Dorothy, *Holbeach Past* (1988)

Clark, Bernard, *Spalding in Early Victorian Times* (Abbey Print, 2005)

Clark, Bernard and Rose, *Spalding in Late Victorian Times* (R. Clark, 2005)

Elsden, Michael J., *Aspects of Spalding Villages* (Bookmark, 2000)

Gooch, E.H., *A History of Spalding* (The Spalding Free Press & Co. Ltd, 1940)

Johnson, Margaret, *History and Photographs of a Spalding Family* (Chris Lane of Artinfusion, 2009)

Leveritt, Norman, & Michael J. Elsden, *Aspects of Spalding 1790-1930* (Chameleon International, 1986)

Leveritt, Norman, & Michael J. Elsden, *Aspects of Spalding – People & Places* (Chameleon International, 1989)

Pursglove, Rosalyn, *A Postcard from Spalding* (The Kings England Press, 1992)

Archaeological Project Services Building Report (June 1999): Ayscoughfee Hall

Websites:

https://sites.google.com/site/hauntedspaldingbook (This website contains extra features connected to the book, such as audible EVP and further photographs)

http://www.ayscoughfee.org (Details of Ayscoughfee Hall investigation nights can be found via this link)

www.paranormaldatabase.com/lincolnshire

http://www.mysticalblaze.com/GhostsNature.htm

http://www.ourcuriousworld.com

If you enjoyed this book, you may also be interested in...

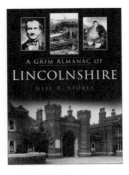

A Grim Almanac of Lincolnshire

NEIL R. STOREY

This day-by-day catalogue of 365 ghastly tales from around the county explores th darker side of Lincolnshire's past. Including diverse tales of highwaymen, smuggler giants, hangmen, poachers, witches, rioters and rebels, and also featuring accounts of prisons, punishments, dreadful deeds, macabre deaths, strange occurrences and heinous homicides, the nasty goings-on of Lincolnshire's yesteryear are all here.

978 0 7524 5768 0

Murder & Crime Lincolnshire

DOUGLAS WYNN

The historic city of Lincoln has a history going back to the Romans and a catalogue of crimes to match. John Haigh, the 'Acid Bath Murderer', was born in nearby Stamford and was imprisoned in Lincoln – where he experimented on sm animals to perfect his acid-bath techniques. The city also has its share of women who drowned unwanted babies, and husbands who beat their wives to death. Combining meticulous research with evocative photography, the author provides feast of crime to haunt the imagination.

978 0 7524 5921 9

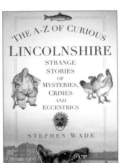

The A-Z of Curious Lincolnshire:
Strange Stories of Mysteries, Crimes and Eccentrics

STEPHEN WADE

Filled with hilarious and surprising examples of folklore, eccentrics, and historical and literary events, all taken from Lincolnshire's tumultuous history, the reader will meet forgers, poets, aristocrats, politicians and some less likely residents of the county, including Spring-Heel'd Jack and the appearance of an angel in Gainsborough. This is the county that brought us Lord Tennyson, John Wesley, an the notorious hangman William Marwood.

978 0 7524 6027 7

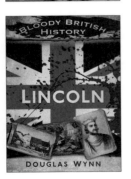

Bloody British History: Lincoln

DOUGLAS WYNN

Built by the Romans, looted by the Danes and conquered by King William I (wh devastated the town to build a castle and a cathedral), the city of Lincoln has had a long and most dreadful history. This book contains medieval child murder, vile sieges, the savage repression of the Lincolnshire rising, and plagues, lepers, prisons riots, typhoid, tanks and terrible hangings by the ton – you'll never see the city i the same way again.

978 0 7524 6289 9

Visit our website and discover thousands of other History Press books.

www.thehistorypress.co.uk

The Histor Press